THE

# CHANGE

R. Michael Buck

**Acknowledgements:**

I need to thank….


My wife, Sandy for offering me the time and freedom to be able to do this. I get lost at times as I write, and she never waivers. She treats me like a King, and I love her for it.


My friends Marilyn Cramp and Sarah Helland and her daughter Geneva for volunteering their time to read the initial copy of this book before it reached a good point. They offered me confidence and support to continue


. Thank you

# THE CHANGE

**2040:**

The morning seemed to begin as any other since the war. For Charlie, consciousness came slowly and his body anticipated the cold and dreariness. It had railed against the early morning pains for many previous mornings stretching back farther than he wanted to remember. Finding a good reason to move still remained a priority and each day it became a fraction harder with new aches and pains of mid-life. Within the darkness, the cool wind brought the smell of fresh burning wood through the many small holes in his small one man teepee. Charlie knew that someone, probably Gloria, had already started the breakfast fires.

He slowly threw a leg out from under his multi-color rag woven blanket and over the edge of the two foot high stack of brown boxing material he had collected as a bed and slowly stood.

*If It wasn't for the rats and snakes, I'd throw half of that pile away and sleep on the ground,* he thought.

His back creaked and grumbled at him with his early morning stretching but he knew after a couple of minutes of movement, it would subside and his 42 year old body would be able to navigate around again with his usual ease. He followed his stretches with twenty jumping jacks and dropped down to do twenty pushups all the while, thinking of times long gone by. This had been a routine of his since long before everything changed.

Finishing the push-ups, he swung his feet under and sat on the floor continuing to stretch his arms over his head; first the left and then the right, reaching as high as he could grabbing the elbow with his other hand. Leaning into the stretch, he felt the muscles in his side pull from his armpit to his hip. He heard a couple of his vertebras crack in that way they sound when you hear it inside your head from the back of your brain.

Finishing his morning workout, he sat back and closed his eyes to thank God for another day and think about Jenna. In another time, he would have been thinking about work, but here, another day of survival had begun, so he started it like all the others and tried to think of happy times gone by.

Finishing his prayers, Charlie looked over toward the still glowing coals from last night's fire. Taking a deep breath he leaned in close to the white powdery residue. He blew a long steady stream of air until the small black coals underneath began coming back to life. The small flame quickly began licking lazily at the morning cold as he slowly added a few small dried twigs, and a few leaves he had collected two days ago in a dry cave. Instantaneously everything began smoking as the fire began to thrive again.

He added a medium log to the infant fire from the stacked pile he had lining the outer edge of the teepee. The warmth would soon spread throughout his home as the sounds of the small crackling fire and the first noise of humanity came with his first rational morning thoughts.

Charlie stepped over to open the leather flap which separated his now warming living space from the cool morning openness of the village compound. Looking out into the spring morning haze, he realized something strangely different was happening. Blinking and not quite understanding what he was seeing, he stepped from his teepee cautiously yet instinctively grabbing the long stake that opened the high upper flap. Flipping the flap that would control the temperature inside the tent, he looked around the village seeing many others doing the same. All of the while the discussions were on "How strange everything seemed, so clear and bright."

The grey shadows which normally entwined the encampment didn't seem the same; everything was sharp and crisp like the morning air. Usually dark and more foreboding, the morning today seemed warm in comparison. Bit by bit Charlie began to realize that all of the typical sounds of the village held an inexhaustible excitement. Charlie too, felt the excitement growing inside as he began to realize this would be a good day, a very good day indeed.

As Charlie was beginning to awake, Maria also began her day. Looking around, she found her younger sister standing just outside the door flap looking up at the horizon.

"What, are you doing?" she asked her. "The morning hasn't even begun shining through the clouds yet; why are you out here? You know how dangerous it is outside before the dawn and dad isn't even home!"

When no response came back, Maria questioned, "Harriett?"

"Something is strangely different." Harriett replied to her older sister, "I can feel it! Look there," indicating toward the horizon, "Something is in the air and the sky seems different, but I can't put my finger on it!"

"Finger on it," Maria spat back, "You better get inside before a dog pack, or worse some scavenger, comes by and checks you out for a breakfast snack or some light morning entertainment" "Now, get inside Harriet!"

The two sisters, Maria just turning seventeen and Harriett, fourteen, were both well trained in survival in their harsh environment. They turned and swung the high upper flap open. Getting out of the strange morning glow, Maria quizzically closed the door flap. Turning toward the east and looking at the horizon, she noticed that maybe Harriett was right! Something did seem different out there!

Inside their large open teepee, the thick smell of the open fire Harriett started earlier filled the lungs of the girls as they began their morning chores. After picking up the sleeping area, they shook out the small skin rugs that lay on the much larger overlapping floor hides that form the base of the Tee Pee. They cleaned out the left over ashes from last night's fire and finally started warming the left over water from yesterday's trip to the spring. They worked quietly awaiting the sound of their father and the other hunters returning home from their nighttime hunt.

A time later Maria began "Harriett, the dish water is ready."

"What do you mean, I did the dishes yesterday morning!" she reflexively responded

"YEESSS, but remember I cleaned that stinky old hide dad found yesterday and you said you would do the dishes for the week if I cleaned it." Maria got a look of disgust on her face as she remembered the experience. "You said the whole week, remember."

Harriett involuntarily rolled her upper lip just thinking about the smell it left in their home all day.

Immediately she said, "OK, you're right, anything to keep away from that thing." and she began putting the few dirty dishes they had in the metal tub of hot water. She was careful remembering the countless times she had burned her fingers in the boiling water.

After what seemed a short time, they heard the familiar entry call for the Rock Valley Village and they felt an excitement run through the entire community.

"Hey Yo, to all inside!" one of the returning hunters yelled at the outer wall.

That was their father's voice and they both quickly finished what they were dong and headed to the Teepee opening!

"Hey Yo, Ho to all who enter", was replied back from the Wall Watchers to the returning men.

Like most villages, the Rock Valley Village was built with two walls. The Outer Wall consisting of long sharpened spear shaped rods that are only spaced two inches apart. This entire wall was built angled away from the inner Tall Wall at the correct height to stop any large animal or any stranger from getting into the village.

Specifically it was designed to prevent anyone, friend or foe, from getting very close to the main opening in the Tall Wall. This is the only access to the Village proper

Referred to as the Tall Wall, the inner wall was much higher, at fifteen feet, than the Outer Wall and added a much more comforting level of security. The entry through the small wall was only large enough for two men to pass side by side in full view of the Wall Watchers who stood at the corners of the compound. Consequently, in combination the space between the walls offered a much easier area to defend.

Attached to the Tall Wall was a large bundle of sharpened sticks tied together with a single strand of hemp rope. The long rope which bundled them was also tied to a crossbeam suspended from two long poles on either side of the opening in the Outer Wall. It looks very much like a large simple child's swing only much more dangerous.

With the cut of the holding rope, the bundle would swing into the opening in the Outer Wall to completely block it. Anyone trying to enter without permission or anything standing in its way as it traveled the short but lethal arc would be killed. When it completed the arc, it would be wedged tightly into the opening adding full security

The fifteen foot Tall Wall was planted in the ground another six feet and twenty feet behind the Outer Wall. Depending upon the village, most defensive walls were built from large logs cut similar to how those of an old Wild West fort would have been done. It was the last line of protection for the entire village so anyone wishing to enter the village needed to pass muster before entry would be granted through the final main gate and into the village main square; no exceptions.

Entry would only be granted in two important steps.

First every entrant needed to get the attention of the Wall Watchers. This was done by yelling the call. By the time the Wall Watchers recognize them with a return call, they had already been under surveillance for some time; usually before they even reached the Outer Wall in the first place

Sentinels were placed in ambush positions in the surrounding area that only the members of the Village Council knew about. Working in pairs, they served a lonely job spending 24 hour shifts sitting outside the walls every three days. Changing only during the night hours, they left and returned home with the Hunters each day.

Through the use of secret communications, they kept the Wall Watchers informed if anyone strange was in the area. The girls once heard that their father had found some special glasses called Night Vision Glasses for the village and with them, the Sentinels can see in the dark. Although few had ever seen them, everyone in the Village was thankful because more than once, sentinels had kept a Scavenger away, or saved someone from The Scrounge.

Many speculated that the communications was done by a "tech" that was left over from the old days; the days before the destruction. But only those involved actually understood and they weren't talking.

"Hey, Yo", came a yell again from the Hunters signaling the Wall Watchers that all was well and they belonged to the village. Entry was finally granted. This same process was used with everyone, friend or stranger, no exceptions.

Their father, who serves as the Security Elder of the village, had told the girls that each village has their own special greeting at the Outer Wall. Because of this, all Wall Watchers know immediately if those asking entry are really strangers, or possibly someone returning after a long absence. Anyone not offering the correct greeting is forced to wait beyond the Outer Wall while the 4 Village Elders are notified.

In the Rock Valley Village age is respected and each Elder meets age requirements for their positions. Charlie is the Chief Elder and at 42 is just at the required 40 years. Their Dad, Bill, is second in charge as the Security Elder and is 50. He will be replaced at 60 by a younger man at least 45. Miss Sara, 60, is the Elder of the Faithful and has been in her position since turning 50. She will remain in her position until she decides to pass it along. She maintains the moral codes based upon faith in God and understands the laws within the village. She serves with Charlie as one of the two judges of the village.

Lastly, Sam, 30, is the Youth Elder having just been selected only a year ago. He is still learning his position as he attends all of the Elders gatherings. Someday, he is to become the next Elder of the Faithful, or Chief Elder depending upon his abilities and the selection of the villagers. Their dad will be replaced by one of the Protectors who are the warriors of the village. They are also the Wall Watchers, the Sentinels or the Hunters.

Beyond the Elders, there were three Elders in Training. They are each assigned to follow an Elder every other day, but only as observers. They have no voting rights or abilities to add to the discussions pertaining to the Village. Adding to their Wisdom and Moral direction will help them become Elders themselves with time and age.

They are usually in their twenties, but Maria had been selected just a month ago because of her work with the children of the village. She was teaching the young ones to read and how to add and subtract for two hours a day. This released many of the women to help in other ways around the village, and gave all of the young children a place to show their special skills. Some would show skills that would lead them to become Elders, Teachers for special programs, Hunters or Protectors.

This morning, the hunters were quickly allowed into the village, and the families began the welcoming ceremonies. Women were overjoyed to see their husbands come home, and young children ran to greet their dads. Yesterday's Sentinels gave a report to the Elders and early morning in the village began.

Return of the hunters meant, the women would shortly be preparing food and the village breakfast would soon be served. The girls could already taste the rich flavors of the fresh wild game.

The Village had collected their own chickens and cows for eggs and milk, but the meat needed to be game Beef was too precious to use as meat protein.

There was a time when it was very dangerous to be a Hunter outside the village. Right after the desolation, game was difficult to find, and great distances were traveled to hunt. Competition with the Forest City Village to the east caused such difficulty that the squabbling finally escalated enough that it lead to the death of a Hunter competing over a rabbit.

Five years ago Charlie and Bill decided enough was enough and together they traveled the sixty mile journey to the Forest City Village and offered a solution to the long dispute.

 Since then the game was getting more prevalent and the hunters no longer had small skirmishes over the rights to fallen game.

Together they established no-hunt zone which Forest City and Rock Valley Hunters do not enter. These areas have allowed the wild game a free range area to procreate and therefore increase the availability of game for both villages. Soon there was plenty of game again, and there was no need to compete against each other.

Since that time, the two Villages have worked in harmony to improve the entire area. Villagers can now travel from one village to the other to visit friends with only a short clearance time before entry. To everyone in both villages, this meant ample fresh food, expanded friendships and increased marrying partners. All adding to the safety, health and stability of both villages.

Last year the two villages established teams of "Communicators" who run between villages with information, letters or vital messages from leadership. These men are recognized by both villages and offer warnings between villages as well as personal connection. Travel has improved since the first meetings, but sadly anyone traveling outside any village must still be alert for Scavengers, Scrounge, and larger wild animals like the dog packs or the big cats!

Their Dad dropped his quiver and Long Bow outside the tent and removed his hunting moccasins before opening the teepee door.

"Hi gorgeous; Dad's home." He smiled at Maria as his head pushed inside the flap door. Maria gave him a huge smile and continued her chores.

"Where's my best little girl?" he said overlooking Harriett on purpose.

She ran to his arms and gave him a huge warming hug that gave them both a feeling of love and satisfaction. Harriett had been blessed with the long blond hair and deep blue eyes he spent many nights staring into when he and their mother would gaze at each other following a long busy day. She made Bill's heart jump with joy every time she was around.

Maria had been blessed with the dark brown curly hair and green eyes that Bill remembered as a boy when his mother pulled him close. Her rugged beauty had been typical of his family. But seeing the girls' together everyone is surprised to learn they are sisters.

Bill always held deep in his thoughts the two women who were most important in his other life, but here his two daughters were his first and only cause. They know instinctively that he would gladly give his life for either of them, and so did he.

He handed Maria a small bag that was glistening wet with the blood from the freshly killed small animal inside followed by another hug. Maria knew that her dad had made the first kill that night because this was a small portion of the meat given for making that kill. Everything else that the hunters brought down would be shared at the communal meals over the next two days in the village Long House.

Harriett hurried across the teepee and received the skin he had over his shoulder. That skin always contained the few greens and any vegetables he had collected along the way. When they opened the second bag, and saw wild onions and morel mushrooms from the wild forest, they both knew

that Raccoon was on the menu today. Mushrooms and wild onion were always served with raccoon.

After removing what they needed for now, Harriett took the skin out the front flap of the teepee to put the extra vegetables in the cold cellar their dad had dug the previous summer. Suddenly, with a long and stunned "WOW" she almost immediately jumped back inside. Both Maria and her father were startled by her actions and gave her a look of surprise.

"Look outside", was all she said as she stood motionless in the doorway.

"What's the matter?" Bill said as he grabbed his survival knife from the leather scabbard next to his sleeping skin.

"Nothing's wrong dad, just look outside!" Harriett said with a strangeness in her otherwise mellow voice.

Maria and her Dad slowly went to the door of the tent and joined Harriett starring out at the scene before them. They were watching the entire encampment become bathed in a light brighter than they had seen in ten years.

## Necessities:

Bill was a large robust man who liked to claim his Scottish background. Often running around in a self-made kilt, it was to anyone's dismay should they comment on his legs. His broad heavy muscular shoulders and arms left no doubt that he would be a formidable adversary in any battle, however, the strong quick head on his shoulders, made people respect the entire man. His only fault was a quick temper that never hesitated in voicing an aggressive opinion; usually the right one.

The Villagers came to accept and respect him and his "moods" because he had become such an integral part at the startup of The Village. Charlie became Chief Elder only because he seemed to be the only man in the village who would stand up to Bill.

Ten years ago, Charlie had been such a calming personality that even Bill recognized his leadership abilities. Charlie was recommended for the position by Bill.

"Look, the day will come," Bill told the others "when a Military Leader will be needed, but to run this village, you will need a negotiator with a cool head. I am not a negotiator and there are times when I don't always keep a cool head." Some in the crowd chuckled at that comment. Bill smiled and continued. "That job needs skills that I don't have." Standing in front of the entire village, he then placed Charlie's name as his first choice and that endorsement made Charlie the Chief Elder on the first ballot.

As the village established itself and security became a necessity, Charlie recommended other Elder positions. Bill was unanimously given the duty of village Security Elder. After leading them through a number of battles with roving bands of Scrounge and dealing with several Scavenger rapists that had come to the village from Chicago. He organized the men and established a fighting force to protect the others. He immediately had the support of everyone in the village.

Rumor had it that in the early years after the destruction, Bill had spent time traveling. This gave him knowledge of how other early villages worked. It was no surprise it was his idea when their village adopted the secret greeting similar to those used by other villages to help increase security.

Even before he was elected Security Elder, the other men of the village, especially the Hunters, respectfully called him Colonel as a sign of leadership. Because he was the only one in the village who had actually served a term in the military the term seemed appropriate.

Usually keeping quietly to himself, and his girls, he accepted the stories about his possible battle experiences without response, but mostly, beyond what people could actually see about Bill, he kept his past life to himself.

He brought the girls here when they were very young. After he met the first group of wanderers who would eventually help establish the Rock River Village. They stayed with the group because of the girls and Bill's need for someone to help in keeping them safe and assisting with their rearing.

As much as anyone knew, Bill's wife had died only a short time earlier due to pneumonia. The girls were immediately befriended by a young mother and her husband whose own daughter had died shortly after the destruction.

Gloria and Sam became very close to Bill and the girls often spent most of their time together. Sam would eventually become the Newest Elder and Gloria became a substitute older sister for the girls. She offered them a motherly ear to talk girl talk.

Bill felt blessed to have them.

Since Bill became the Security Elder, all New Comers are always met with speculation and distrust by the village. Bill, as Security Elder and a group of Protectors go out to meet and establish preliminary talks with anyone new. They bring requests back inside the inner wall to the ruling

Elders who would ultimately be the ones to decide what to do.

Everyone coming to the Outer Wall is offered food and water as an offering of good will and friendship while they wait. If they are refused entrance for any reason and asked to leave the area, once again they are given enough food and fresh water. This time enough for two days travel. They are then allowed twelve hours to leave the area without any repercussions.

However, failure to leave within twenty-four hours, would cause the Protectors to take up arms against the intruders and remove them from the space claimed by the village. This space is clearly marked and claimed at a one click distance around the encampment. Anyone resisting removal from this space would be dealt with swiftly and harshly; up to and including death. Bodies were never buried, but left to serve as a warning to other New Comers entering the space.

The Rock River Village had few skeletons hanging in its safe space, but the girls once saw the outskirts of the Indy Village in central Indiana. That village was days away from here, and that distance made the girls feel safer. Dozens of skeletons lined the entire circle they claimed as their safe space and bone piles were spaced along the final path leading to the village.

The girls remembered the stories their Dad told of the month's right after the Great Destruction; times which were very harsh before the walls were built. The walls became the only way to survive the Anarchists or Scrounge as the people began to call them.

Right after the Destruction, the Scrounge were wandering groups of individuals who began living in opposition to anyone desiring order and civilization. Gradually, The Scrounge began grouping together, ultimately calling themselves Bands. Each Band includes many disgusting, vile and often psychologically distressed individuals.

Moving into what was left of the larger population centers The Scrounge survive by stealing what they want, and killing those who get in their way. As years have passed, The Scrounge began plundering small towns or villages that happen to be nearby. Anyone living on their own, outside a village, was and still is always in danger.

Young women and female children are considered plunder and raped, becoming property of the Band. Older women are used as servants for the Scrounge, if they consider them useful enough.

Anyone over 40 is killed as useless and considered too much trouble to assimilate into the Band. Sometimes they are killed quickly and painlessly, and other times brutally; it all depended upon 'The Whim". The Whim is the self-proclaimed leader of the Band. They usually claim to have mystical powers, even though none have ever proven to actually have any more power than anyone else, just more brutality.

After plundering most of the larger cities and suburban areas, the Scrounge began to travel in smaller easily controlled groups. The Whim and seven to eight soldiers called Wetbacks travel as a front group to find unsuspecting villages.

Once they do a preliminary inspection of a possible place to plunder's defenses, they leave to bring back the rest of the Band. As always, if opportunity avails itself, they destroy and assimilate everything, and anyone they come in contact with.

Some of the Scrounge learned how to produce a low grade blasting powder that is somewhat effective on the Outer Walls of a Village, but has little or no effect on the very thick and strong Tall Walls.

Often they use the powder just for fun by blowing up useless buildings, cars, or anything else they feel should become entertainment for the group. Often a few of the Scrounge themselves become part of the entertainment for the others. Any member who shows empathy, weakness or reach the age of forty may find themselves locked in one of the cars, or buildings to enhance the fun for the rest of the troupe.

It didn't take long before the common survivors realized they needed to gather together and soon the Villages were formed. Villages of enough individuals to ward off The Scrounge Bands, and walls strong enough to offer safety and security from anything The Scrounge might try.

However, the Scrounge are not the only individuals the villages need to worry about.

There are others living alone who sometimes gain entry into the village by lying their way in. Scavengers, named such because that's what they are, live alone and use trickery and lies to gain what they want. Often they are older and have snuck away from a Band before they were killed. They come to a village offering a story that sounds real, but once inside they take advantage of anyone they can. They especially mark single women, young girls or females who have children and no husband. They gain their trust and then steal their food, water and often times their dignity. Some have even tried to steal stored village supplies.

Some try to upset the established order of the village by in-sighting riots. Once they have done their worst, and chaos covers their treachery, they sneak out of the Village taking along their plunder. Any Scavenger allowed inside and found later as untrustworthy is dealt with severely by the Elders.

The girl's dad, Bill, is considered one of the best Security Elders throughout the Northern Illiana Region which includes the Rock Valley Village and 10 other Villages spread across what used to be Northern Illinois and Northern Indiana. Unlike some other villages, the Rock Valley Village is a free zone. Everyone is allowed to exercise their freedom as they please; as long as your idea of freedom doesn't entangle with the freedom of another.

If you are not a village member and you break the rules, you will be killed immediately and left just outside the village walls for the varmints to eat. In the case of one Scavenger, the offence had been so offensive, the rape of a little girl, that the man was hung on the Outer Wall alive. The man screamed hysterically most of the night and in the morning the Hunters cut down what was left of the body, dragging it off into the woods.

The screaming had caused so much discourse in the village that Charlie, as the Village Chief, and Sara as Elder of the Faithful proclaimed that unless someone could give them a good reason, they would never do that again. The screams had been so chilling, no-one disagreed; even Bill.

Village members who broke the rules would be brought to Charlie and Sara to proclaim judgment and sentencing. If the village member demanded "audience", Charlie would gather all of the elders together as a jury to listen to the charges and the defense of the member.

As a group, they hear the evidence and together they accept or void the judgment given earlier.

In most of these cases, banishment was the punishment and the accused would be sent from the village safe zone. They would need to connect with another village, but that was often very difficult and years could pass before another village accepted them as a member.

But this day the whole village had dreamed of since the Great Destruction. After all the waiting it was finally here.

The girls stood there in awe inspired excitement, and Bill began to cry quietly letting the tears openly run down his cheeks. It had been so long!!

**Today:**

The joy of astounded disbelief grew into loud laughter and excited shouts as the entire village moved into the center of the encampment to enjoy the fullness of the moment. Everyone was hugging and cheering as the first real sunrise in 10 years slowly crept across the horizon and spread out across the sky.

Charlie moved toward the flag pole which centered the Village clearing and just stared at the sheer beauty of the moment. Tears were streaming down his face as he and many others began removing their shirts to feel the sun's rays rest upon their chest and arms. It was as if he was being reborn.

 Looking around, he could see the rest of the villagers uncovering their skin as modestly as possible, but to open their senses to the sun's rays was irresistible. He felt the warmth of the sun spreading across his being and he felt better than he could remember in a long, long time.

It was just a few minutes later when he heard Sara and Sam commence the first prayers of thanksgiving being raised to God. Through word stopping awe, he let his voice join in the praise being raised to the Great Spirit, Jehovah, for the return of the sun.

The Sunshine, the warmth, the future.

The moment became reality as the Villagers slowly dropped to the ground with the "Prayer of the Fathers", spoken as they remembered it passed year after year through all of the villages;

"Our Father in Heaven, Great be thy name……

Charlie knew they would not be alone in their praise for the day, and finally there seemed hope for the future.

With it, the sunshine brought dreams of a true harvest and agriculture that had only been foraging before. If the sun continues coming up each morning they could begin the rebirth of farming, fruit trees, maybe even fishing could be reestablished.

The land that had been destroyed during the Great Destruction could finally return. With an increase in natural vegetation there would be more wildlife to hunt. More wildlife, and agriculture means a return of overall health. Yes this was an exceptionally good and hopeful morning!

Through his joy, Charlie allowed his mind return to the days before the great destruction. A time, he knew too many of the young people here would only have vague flashes in their earliest memories. *How it used to be.* He thought.

No-one during that life and especially Charlie would ever have believed all that had happen over these this decade, and mostly that they seem to have survived.

"Praise God" he said aloud.
 "Praise God" he yelled at the top of his voice.

**The Time Before:**

In the Oval Office, the speaker phone began to beep softly. It was a beautiful November morning in Washington. The sun was shining, the temperature was a warming 50 degrees, and the trees were losing those last few leaves that seemed to hold on for dear life at the end of limbs awaiting for the winter chill. The grass had a gorgeous green that only comes this late in the season, and the political excitement caused by the Presidential Election that was held yesterday was all but gone. They lost.

"Mr. President, William Crest is on the phone sir. He says he needs to see you today, to begin the changeover process."

President Williams was sitting at his desk with both hands over his face and laughed out loud thinking to himself *"They can't even wait one day?"*

Looking up at the staff who sat in front of him, he said "Sure, have the anxious little twerp come around two. Tell him to come alone. I don't think I could handle all of them in the same meeting, Crest will be bad enough. I'll get around to the President Elect later."

Yes, Mr. President." The voice over the intercom said, and a click was heard ending the conversation.

Turning from the phone he wondered how President Elect Phillips could have decided to take Crest as his personal White House Council; he is such a crass individual with a vocabulary that belonged on a ditch digger, not a Senator.

Getting up from his chair across from the President, Vice President Paul Miday picked up his glass, grabbed some ice and reached for the Kentucky Bourbon bottle on the table between himself and Ed Bloom, the head of the Republican Party.

"Well, this day couldn't get any better, could it? Miday remarked as he poured a shot into his glass. 'Why couldn't they just wait one day, just 24 hours before they begin their, Change Again?"

Miday sputtered some more to himself as he flopped on the couch.

"Look," Senator Ed Bloom started, "Personally, I don't want to see any of them. You guys do what you think is best". Bloom had supported the President through both the first and now the second campaign and held a huge disgust for the new President Elect and his team.

Everyone in the room turned toward Ed as he continued, "We know what they want, and honestly I'm inclined to let them have it. I understand that you don't agree Paul, but this battle is over Mr. President. Let's just lick our wounds and leave with our dignity.

"Your right, I don't agree." Vice President Miday sputtered. "We have this administration for another two months, and we should keep it right up until the last minute." He took a drink from his glass. "We can help in the transition and make it amiable, but I do not think we need to give up the ship. Mr. President, you are going to be the scapegoat for everything that happens from now until the inauguration. You need to keep control!"

From across the room, another shape took a sip from a glass of coke and chimed in "They promised that we would look the same, smell the same and taste the same as we have this past year. It seems they just want the last word in making any final decisions. Anthony Brusch walked over and put his hand on the Presidents shoulder.

"Look my friend, I have supported you financially all the way here. We have accomplished some amazing things, but today you look tired. I know you feel cheated by not getting a second term, but time will come to your defense as it sorts out the truth." Tony, as the President knew him, sat in a chair more centrally located in the discussion; crossed his legs and sipped his coke. "As more truth from these last four years becomes available to the public and more is told about the Democrats and their "Billion Dollar Club" the country will look differently on you and your term in office.

You know and I know that Phillips and the Democrats can't do everything he threatened. They don't control the Senate or the House." Shaking his head and taking another long sip, he let it slowly trickle down the back of his throat enjoying the cool iciness as it relaxed him. Looking up he continued "I don't think the citizens of the USA will let that happen again after 08."

"I have to agree, hon." A female voice added from the back of the room. "You look very tired today and God knows it's been a long hard fight. You have been criticized from the moment you were elected until now. Let this new guy catch some heat." The First Lady, Mrs. Williams, smiled at her husband from an overstuffed chair in the back corner of the room.

The President knew that if he did what Crest and President Elect Phillips were asking, he was promised a good place in history. Besides the old Democratic guard wouldn't let him do anything anyway, these last few months seemed to be useless.

He now understood the idea of a "lame duck" Presidency.

President Williams smiled as a look of peace came over his face. "I'm tired of the fight, Paul. You have served me well and have been a great friend and support. I couldn't have asked for a better VP. Ed, you have advised me well, but this seems to be my choice and my legacy." Thoughtfully, he said "If I move over now we won't be missing anything.

"We all know the Democrats in Congress won't allow anything we suggest to pass without Phillips telling them too. By the time the Republicans finally take over, my term will be over. Sorry Paul, I'm going down the hall with my wife to her room and relax for a few weeks."

The Vice President angrily turned and left the room followed at a safe distance by Ed Bloom and Tony Brusch. The President and Mrs. Williams relaxed in the Oval office and waited alone quietly for two o'clock to come.

At exactly 2:00 a light knock was heard at the door as it creaked open. A soft female voice announced "Mr. President, Mr. Crest is here sir. He's accompanied by President Elect Phillips."

President Williams smiled at the First Lady as she snuck out of the room through the back door. He took a deep breath and prepared himself for what he knew would be a meeting from hell!

## August:

When the alarm began beeping the young man stretched his long and fit arms above his head pushing against the headboard like he did every morning. Giving a groan, and quickly shutting his eye lids, he realized the sun was shining directly in his eyes through the wide windows that lined their tenth story apartment.

The sun was almost too bright in the clear morning sky as it came as a laser through the large window of their bedroom. Usually they closed the curtains before going to bed. Squinting with one eye, he rolled over as he began talking.

"Honey, would you, please, turn off the alarm sometime soon?" the young man said continuing to roll feeling for his wife.

*Oh yeah*, he hazily remembered, *she left early this morning for LA. She opened the curtains! I'll have to pay her back for this one."*

Charlie stretched across the bed and slapped at the alarm clock almost knocking it off the glass topped nightstand as the loud beeping finally stopped. Lying back on the bed he wished he could stay, but he knew that was not an option.

Sitting up, he swung his feet over the edge of the bed and just sat there. He rubbed his eyes and extended the rub down the full length of his face by opening his hands. He thought how good it felt as he began a deep long yawn. Taking a long deep breath in through his nose, he held it for a few seconds before he slowly allowed it to escape out of his mouth. Raising his hands above his head he stood and reached for the ceiling allowing the stretch to press a loud sigh from his chest. Dressed in the black silk sleeping pants Jenna had bought him last Christmas, he bent over to do a toe touch, and thought *"that's enough"*.

If Jenna were here she would already have two miles in on the treadmill, and insist that he do those 15 bends and 20 push-ups. He smiled to himself as he sat on the bed again. Still not totally awake, he rose and wandered off to the shower dropping his sleeping pants on the way looking forward to the cool shower. He walked by Jenna's full length mirror and after a short stop he shook his head and started doing the 15 toe touches. *I hate love handles,* he thought as he started the first one.

Finishing the twenty push-ups, he grabbed the universal remote and turned on the TV for his usual morning noise. Fox News Morning show came on with the usual trio of hosts talking news and sometimes nonsense. Normally he really didn't listen to most of the sound, but this morning they seemed more intense than usual. He stopped for a moment and thought how the two guys were ok but the blond! *Fox sure gets its share of good looking ladies to do their news,* he thought. Suddenly the actual story broke through his day dreaming and stopped him in his tracks.

"The shot had been fired from the area around the Washington Monument." were the words that he heard, and he forgot all about the shower as he pulled his pants back on without dropping his gaze.

He sat back down on the edge of the bed and watched the world change before his eyes.

## Begin:

5:30 AM....President Phillips had already called an early morning meeting with his staff in the oval office. A year and a half into his first term, surrounded by his closest advisors, and he still found himself amazed that he was actually here. All the planning, all the maneuvering, and all the lying had all been worth the trouble. He almost laughed when he remembered back to those first days in Iowa when everyone had told him how impossible this was. He never forgot other candidates snickering at him as they counted their chickens before they hatched. He especially remembered William Crest coming up to him after he won that first caucus, looked him in the eye and told him "We can do this!"

Now a year and six months into his first term, everything was on the precipice of disaster. As much as he liked this position, everything was not going as planned. He took a sip of his first cup of coffee, puffed the first drag on his cigarette and looked at William Crest's empty chair.

Andy Wallace, the Presidents top advisor next to William Crest and David Andrews the head of the Democratic Progressives for Change who had given Phillips the votes and money to win the election, sat uncomfortably in their chairs waiting for President Phillips to explode in his customary manner when things were not going his way.

"Where is William, Andy?" The President spat.

"Haven't a clue Sir, He usually is the first one here, David, any ideas?" Andy said hoping to turn the attention to David Andrews.

Mumbling, David just threw up his hands, shook his head and grabbed a glazed donut from the coffee table.

Walking around behind his desk, President Phillips looked disgustedly out of the large picture window that graced the space toward the Washington Monument. Looking around out into the darkness that this early part of the day offered, he only had a memory of the beautiful view available from this vantage point. The lights on the mall gave outlines of the buildings and trees, and emphasized the magnitude of the Washington Monument. With the sun still hiding well below the horizon, he wondered what was offering the small glimmer from a distant object low on the other side of the Mall.

Turning toward the others, he loudly proclaimed "It better be important. With all the troubles we have right now William needs to be here. Will never lets these meetings happen without him being here. Something must be wrong!"

Suddenly the door swung opened and slammed against the wall behind it. The entire group jumped and total silence filled the room. William Crest stood in the doorway breathing heavily.

Wondering what was going on, Andy jumped up to see if something happened in the outer office. William continued standing in the door frame with his face pale looking at the others as if the world was ending.

"Mr. President!" William said, with a look of disbelief on his face. "Mr. President, come with me! The rest of you need to get out of here!" he yelled turning toward the rest of the puzzled group.

Two large and frightening FBI agents rushed into the room and grabbed at President Phillips dragging him through the open door, almost knocking William Crest to the floor.

When the rest of the group just stood there and failed to move quickly enough, William used his famous language and said "Get the f—k out of here. There has been a shooting and we all need to move with the President, now!!"

Gathering himself together, he ran out of the room following the FBI agents who were now escorting President Phillips down the hallway.

As the others herded toward the door like lemmings following each other over the cliff, they could hear the President yelling, "Where are we going, Will? Will!!"

It was at that moment a loud dull thud on the other side of the President's desk broke through the noise of moving shuffling feet. David Andrews turned with Andy Wallace just in time to see the window behind the President's desk spider into that unmistakable circle pattern that only leaves safety glass with that little round hole in the center. Two seconds later the second shot completely shattered the window from one side to the other leaving the glass concaved in the middle.

The first shot must have weakened the glass enough for the second, the perfect lucky shot, to pass through the initial hole; a million to one shot.

Some part of David Andrews splattered on the opposite wall as he slumped lazily to the floor, dead.

## Conspiracy:

The shot had seemed impossible to begin with, just hitting the window took superior marksmanship, but placing a second shot on the same trajectory would be a miracle shot. There was really no hope of actually killing the President or anyone else, but that was not the purpose. The message this challenge would send would be louder than any attempted assassination since Booth.

Moving farther up the tree where he could actually see the White House, Billy, looking through the huge hunting scope. He could see the window glass was cracked and shattered like a car windshield hit by a fast moving rock thrown from the tires of another vehicle.

Billy was not disappointed that the glass had stopped the bullets and was still satisfied with himself; he actually hit it.

When his brain suddenly realized the ramifications of the second shot; the dream shot, the shot no one could possibly make, he became terrified. He had hit …….someone.

When he fired it, he had only hoped at best it would completely destroy the window and accentuate the attempt of terrorism. But through the scope, he saw where somebody's blood was running down the back wall of the oval office.

*My God, I did it*! He excitedly thought to himself as he moved out of the tree faster than he had ever attempted before. The idea that he may have actually killed the President brought a new fear into his life.

He thought of his young family. He would be hunted down by everyone except those who were in on the attempt. *They needed to disappear.*

**30 Minutes Ago....**Senator Danvers of Connecticut had just left his home outside Washington and climbed into his black stretch limousine for the ride to the Capital. He grabbed the cup of Starbucks that the driver picked up for him every morning, and began looking over the New York Times. This was the first of the three papers he planned to look over today on the trip in. However, he failed to realize that the driver was not his normal driver. His driver was lying in the trunk with a small hole in his head.

When the safety glass opened and the Senator looked up, he was looking into the barrel of a silencer. He had no time to think. The bullet entered his Starbucks cup and exploded the contents all over the two thousand dollar Armani blue suit the Senator was wearing. The coffee blended with the blood that seeped from the hole over the Senators heart.

The safety glass closed and the Senator would be found four hours later at the airport, still in the back seat holding the paper.

**20 Minutes Earlier….**Senator Walker snuck out of his front door to get the morning paper as he did most mornings. He could feel the crisp chill of the new day as he looked up and down the street. He gazed up at the Moon over the high rise across the street and took a moment to clean his glasses so he could see it better. Dropping his clean white handkerchief on the steps, he quickly bent down to pick it up. With surprise he looked across the quiet street at a bright flash that caught his eye. That instant was the only thing that saved his life as the two bullets splattered on the marble wall inside the entryway. Both bullets had passed through the same air space his torso had filled a second earlier.

**10 Minutes Later….**Speaker of the House Wilson climbed off the military flight at Reagan International Airport. She had just arrived on her routine weekly flight back to Washington grumbling as usual to someone on her cell phone. The Military flight left Oregon four hours earlier, and due to clear skies over the mountains, it had been slightly faster than normal. So she stood waiting impatiently for her Limousine on the tarmac. Her secret service guards would be as happy as she when the limo finally arrived.

"I called you and told you I would be early." She yelled into the phone "Where is he? …….. But he's not here! ………. I pay way too much money to be standing here waiting."

The pilots nodded at her as they began walking the short distance toward the hanger and the Attendant who accompanied the Speaker everywhere, descended the few remaining steps to the tarmac. She plopped herself disgustedly on the lowest step and began looking at her e-mails.

The Secret Service Guard reached into his coat pocket to pull out a cigarette, but quickly returned it as he saw the Congress Women's ire beginning to rise. He knew this was not the time to push the envelope and suffer the unending yelling. He had been here before, so he knew the Speaker could unleash a hail of uncomplimentary language toward anyone at any time, especially when she had to wait for her ride. Smoking would definitely not be allowed today.

The Speaker surprisingly noticed the calmness and the unusually clean smell in the air this early in the day. She closed her eyes enjoying the moment and the unusual warmth the morning was offering. The first shot went unnoticed by her as it hit the guard who needed the cigarette in the head. He dropped like a broken balloon, seeming to float lazily to the ground.

Lifting her eyes when the blood spattered frothily on her face, the Attendant was stunned and frozen with fear. Starring at the guard lying at her feet, she had been a simple target for the second quick shot. Her head snapped back and she slumped forward still sitting on the bottom step.

The Speaker, finally realizing her ride had arrived, died on the shiny black tarmac as her shiny black limousine rolled up for the ride she no longer needed.

The driver side window slowly closed hiding a silencer and 9mm hand gun. In the back of the Limousine sat a silent Senator who had spilled his Starbucks. The Limo quickly left the area.

**Five minutes later....**the President was being dragged from the Oval office, and Andy was dying. Turning only slightly when he heard the glass crack, The President headed down the hallway trusting the FBI officers as he began looked for his family.

Sensing the Presidents concern, one of the officers said, "Mr. President, they will be safe. We had the FBI go for them as soon as we heard the news; Mrs. Phillips and the children are already heading for the bunker!"

For millions of children in the United States another Monday had started another week of school. In and around Washington, as in other communities, big yellow buses were traveling their routes on what will turn out to be a beautiful warm and sun shiny day.

The first of many Out-of-State visitors were just getting off of the subway looking for a restaurant for breakfast as they plan to begin their day of sightseeing in Washington. In a couple hours the doors of the Smithsonian would open to let the first workers in for their shift.

The White stone on the Capital Mall, the Washington Memorial, the Wading Pool full of water stretching from the Lincoln Memorial to the WWII Memorial, all caught the sun light as it crested over the trees lining the Mall. It was starting as just another day, except it would not be just another day.

The New Minutemen had made their statement. Looking at his watch, he knew that by this time the world would know the second American Revolution was real and they were not afraid to take on the most powerful people in the world to keep their freedom.

Billy quickly broke the rifle down. Sliding it into his backpack, he began climbing out of the tree.

Looking up, He saw the police officer coming across the grass. Halfway down, he slowed, but continued the awkward descent to the ground. He pulled his handgun and waited behind the tree. Stepping out from behind the tree he took a deep breath for the first time now that he was sure who was coming.

"How did it go?" the officer asked

Nodding his head, Bill pulled off the one piece gardener's suit he had used to stay clean, and straightened up the police uniform he wore underneath. The two men walked to the edge of the Wadding Pool as if they were doing their normal daily patrol and after looking around, Bill deposited the rifle in the middle. It would take weeks for someone to find it.

At the same time, The President, visibly shaken, relaxed slightly, smiled and climbed out of the elevator that leads to the safety bunker 100 feet below the White House. William Crest climbed out right behind him and the two men calmly walked a short hallway to the bunker. Crest turned to the FBI agents and the Secret Service officers and had them wait outside.

Closing the sound proof door, Crest leaned against it and turned to the President. "Congratulations Sir." Crest said smiling back "I love it when a plan comes together."

Both men laughed and were surrounded by ten other individuals including Mrs. Phillips, and nine other high ranking Progressives from the Congress and Governorships. "High Fives" were sported all around the room. Everyone there understood what had just happened and were well aware of the next move.

"Nothing unnerves a country and its people more than a good old fashioned assassination attempt." William Crest stated loudly.

That had been the statement which rallied the Political Elite into this plan over a year ago.

Following a secret meeting of those families who considered themselves a Royal Class, the nudging began.

Militia meetings were infiltrated, internal terrorists were pin-pointed and assisted as a real plan came together. Those who were not part of the plan and were in positions of power were suggested as "to be eliminated". Those eliminations had happened this morning.

The only problem was that these elitists didn't realize the very real underlying discontent that festered through the middle of the country. They also did not anticipate the resolve and belief of the many Militia organizations.

The forces in office only knew that they could not pass all of their Progressive programs unless they could remain in office, forever. They had maneuvered voting blocks, the underprivileged, the illegal aliens, anyone who felt they were a minority and most of the women's groups. All these groups could now be counted on voting to keep them,

Progressives that is, in office. However, that was not good enough. It would only take one bad election and everything they had worked for would end. That couldn't happen.

So they needed a good reason to declare Martial Law and The Progressives could control the entire country. No one would question their declaration, because the people would be too shocked following these assassinations to question anything. They would want security at any cost.

Now all that was needed was to create uncontrolled panic in the streets and everyone would be too busy trying to survive to worry about Washington.

The American Political Royalty thought everything seemed to be going as planned.

That is until the next shot was fired.

## Flight:

'Hello, anybody home?" Bill called as he entered the house.

"Hi honey, his wife Michelle called from upstairs. What are you doing home early? It's not even ten o'clock; what happened to going in early and working later for the overtime?"

"They decided they didn't need me." He yelled back.

"Is everything okay? Fred's been calling for you since nine. He seems really anxious to talk with you.

Bill walked to the living room and grabbed the house phone from beside his recliner. Dialing the number, he felt anxious about what this conversation was all about.

"Hey Fred; what's happening

"Have you seen the news?" came the voice over the phone.

"No, Why!"

"Man, we're in trouble!"

"What do you mean? Nobody but our group knows anything." Bill walked over to his prized sixty inch flat screen and switched on the local news.

"I don't......oh no!" was Bill's involuntary comment as he realized that much more was going on than any of the militia understood. "What the hell!" Bill said as he hung up the phone without saying anything more to Fred.

Michelle came down the stairs and began cleaning downstairs until Bill yelled at her. "Please Michelle, stop! I need to hear all of this and it might not hurt you to watch too."

"Oh Bill, you know I don't do politics and that stuff you get into."

"No Michelle…this is bad; real bad."

"What do you mean bad?" as she walked into the living room and realized what was on the screen.

The news caster was talking about an attempted assassination of the President and the deaths of three Senators and others. At this time they were not sure exactly how many total were dead in this attempted coup, but the President was fine. Preliminary reports were flying on every channel, but no-one seemed to know the total story.

"Michelle, I need to go out. Now listen to me, closely. Get the girls from school and pack bags for a week. Be sure you have clothes for camping."

"Why Bill? Where are we going? What's this all about?"

"Look Michelle, if the President declares marital Law, we don't want to be anywhere near Washington. Just do what I ask and I'll be back later." Bill grabbed his keys and almost ran out the door. As soon as he jumped into the car, his phone started ringing.

"Yeah Fred I think I get it. We were had! Get everybody together at the safe room and make it in twenty minutes." He ordered. "Look if this is what I think, we are all in too deep to stay. This will put us all in jail for the rest of our lives. Tell them all that this is an order."

Bill backed out of his driveway and drove to the local small airport. Pulling into the drive, he honked his horn for Randy.

"Hey Randy" he yelled at the man who came out of one of the hangers. Randy ran the airport and ran a small side business flying people on trips all over the country. "Are you busy this evening?"

"Nah, not tonight Bill." Randy smiled.

"Can I rent you and your plane for a trip to Cincinnati tonight?

"Tonight? What's going on in Cincinnati that needs you there tonight?"

"A death in the family, my mother's sister."

"Well you better start driving Bill. Nothing is moving anywhere in US airspace unless it has the Air Force insignia on it. We're going under Martial Law."

"Crap." Bill spat. "Never thought they'd do that. When?"

"Rumor has it that the President will take advantage of this opportunity and announce it in the morning."

"OK, I guess I need to rethink my trip."

"Well flying is out." Randy turned to go back to the plane he had been working on.

"What if we fly low; real low?"

Randy stopped and turned around. "Man, in order to fly low enough we'd need to be Angels." Randy put down the wrench he had been using and looked quizzically at Bill. "What did you do?"

Bill turned and started walking away. As he reached his car he stopped. "Bottom line Randy, could you fly my family out of here; I don't care where anymore, just away, and can you do it under the radar and without questions?

Randy looked at Bill for what seemed a long time. "Bill, we went through Iraq together....twice. You were one of the best snipers I've ever heard of; hell you saved my life more than once. You even drank beer with me when no one else would." Randy shifted feet uncomfortably. "As low as we will be, how will your family deal with the ride?

Your girls are really young yet man. Can you get them to sleep? Otherwise they'll be crying and even sick."

"Your sounding like you might do this."

"We will need to fly at night with few lights. I will fly one hour, you decide where within a two hundred mile radius. I'll find an air field where I can stay the night and rent a car. I'll leave the plane and wait for things to relax. But, when I drop you off, we don't know each other, right!"

"Ever?" Bill commented "So you're doing it?"

"Be here at nine. We will leave at nine- thirty. If you're not here, we don't go at all."

Bill walked over to Randy and grabbed his hand for a shake that turned into a shoulder hug. "Thanks man."

"Don't be late, and I never said I wouldn't ask questions. If I'm taking these chances, I'll need some answers." Randy looked Bill in the eye. "I don't like that look Colonel."

Both men turned away and went their own directions. Randy began the task of preparing a plane to take Bill and his family away, and Bill began the task of preparing his friends for what he knew was coming.

**************

"What are you talking about Bill, our plan worked better than we could have hoped for?" A tall older man stated. He was one of ten men who gathered in the basement room of a non-descript two story house located in a non-descript subdivision in Falls Church, Virginia.

"Aren't you listening to the news?" Bill broke in. "This wasn't just us. Others were involved and Senators died. That took planning and we didn't make those kinds of plans." Bill took a drink from a glass of beer he had sitting on the table next to him. "My concern is who coordinated this whole thing and why. If my belief is true, we are all in danger. We all need to leave here tonight. One way or another, someone's going to get arrested and pay for these deaths and whoever started this mess knows we were involved in the White House part."

"AH, you're crazy Colonel! A young well-built man leaned across the table and questioned Bill. "What you're talking is a conspiracy…..of a conspiracy. It would have been planned all along by those we are against; the Government, the Political Royalty. Why would they start a war on themselves?"

"Did they? Look at those who died. They were liabilities and expendable. The only one who died that wasn't planned was David Andrews and I know that for sure. That second shot wasn't supposed to happen." Bill took another drink. "And now, they have an excuse to declare Martial Law." All the men began questioning each other as the meeting started to spiral into confusion.

"Stop!" Bill shouted into the noise again. "According to rumors, that happens tomorrow morning." The men grew very pensive and looked to Bill. "I learned before coming here that all air flights have been cancelled already. It almost seems that someone wants to keep us here a while longer so they can….." Bill noticed the news on the television. "Turn that volume up, would you?"

The anchor was talking over pictures that depicted the events of the day. "Two Senators, and the Speaker of the House were killed when the government came under attack by Militia groups from around the country this morning." The commentator looked up, smiled at the camera and continued. "A third Senator and The White House were also attacked by what seems to have been a single sniper located on the Mall. This attack resulted in the death of the Presidents long time council and mentor, David Andrews."

"How do they know that much? I mean, the news already? They shouldn't be able to know we're Militia...or any Militia had anything to do with this. On the news, not yet." The tall slender man exclaimed and looked at Bill. Worry was in his eyes as well as the other men in the room. "They'll be after us.....all! Why did you kill Andrews?" he exclaimed threateningly.

Silence filled the room as all eyes settled on Bill.

"We all knew what we were getting into when we sent Bill out this morning. Bill just got lucky." Another voice broke in belonging to an old man who joined in the conversation from a back corner of the room. Continuing, he criticized. "You idiots better not get cold feet now, the mission is done. We are all implicated and you better get that idea through your heads. We knew the consequences and Bill's right. We've been taken in. They know who we are and if they want, where to find us. When they catch us, we'll pay the price."

"You really believe that General?" The young man asked pensively.

"I can't remember a time Bill had it wrong. We need to take action tonight or get rounded up like a bunch of mice for extermination. I know I'm heading north to Canada as soon as this meeting is over. We all have "bug out" plans and I believe it's time to put them to use."

"What do you think Bill?" another asked.

"The General has it right. It has been a pleasure to serve with each of you. Maybe we'll meet again someday."

Raising his glass Bill looked at them all. "May the wind be at you back and peace be your future." Taking his glass and emptying it, he threw it against the concrete wall.

"Good evening gentlemen and keep your families safe. Here is hoping we meet again." Bill saluted the General, turned and headed up the basement steps. He could hear them one by one beginning to say their goodbyes and smashing their glasses as he had done.

Bill climbed into his car and pulled away from the house knowing that tomorrow would bring more surprises. He could see other cars pulling away in his mirror, but he also noticed the quiet that had begun to cover the city. *Is this the calm before the storm he wondered?*

## Martial Law

Americans awoke to the sound of tanks, large Military trucks and even Air Force jets flying overhead in almost every town and city across the country. Overnight, less than 24 hours after the murders and assassination attempts, President Phillips declared Martial Law.

His televised speech cited Anarchy, Home Grown Terrorists, Suicide Bombers and Militia Groups as a need to take full control of the country's law enforcement agencies.

He sent out orders that all military units would report to their home bases. All National Guard Units, State Units and Regular Military were put on twenty four hour duty and subsequently were being sent into almost every town and city throughout the country.

Every Governor was ordered to support the efforts with their State Police Units while Local Police were ordered to stand down. This gave all authority over to the Federal Government.

By the end of that first day, blood shed had already occurred in a few small towns outside Chicago, St. Louis and Houston. Wyoming was threatening revolution with Montana and the Dakota's ready to join in. Texas, supported the other revolting states but not to be outdone, declared they were an independent country and immediately filed papers to secede from the United States.

In Washington, everything that was supposed to be smooth and simple, quickly went into disarray and panic mode. Phillips had not expected so strong an opposition to his declaration, and threatened to use Military force against any state, city, or town that questioned his authority in this situation. He demanded that the State Police take charge in controlling the citizens individually, and instructed the FBI to take charge of the State Police Units.

Scrambling for capitulation from the states, he sent armed military to stand at the Governor's offices in every state that questioned his actions. He demanded their support and promised harsh repercussions if they failed to do so.

Eight Governors were shown on the evening news being hand cuffed and escorted from their offices.

It became quickly apparent that without backing down, the country would fall into chaos.

And Chaos is exactly what happened

## Connecting:

Charlie called Jenna that first morning and after a short conversation discussing what had just happened, he offered to fly to California so they could be together.

Calling in sick, Charlie continued watching the news throughout the early morning as he began packing. He called and reserved a ticket to California for the next morning and made his plans to leave the city. However, as more and more information came across the wires he knew this was going to be bad and at 3:00 in the morning, as he prepared to leave his apartment Charlie understood that traveling by plane would be very difficult, however he still hoped it would not be impossible.

Within an hour, he realized that Martial Law was actually declared and there was no air travel at all. Every non-government or military plane flight was grounded over the continental United States until further notice.

Charlie was grounded and Jenna was stuck in California unless they drove across country to meet each other. Charlie picked up his phone and they made plans

*****************

"Colonel, this is the Lead." The first vehicle in their 50 vehicle convoy called. Each of the units had received orders long before the sun passed the backside of the planet and they hit the road within the hour. This combination of units from Chicago, Rockford and some units from Southern Wisconsin, converged in Bloomington, Illinois at noon, and headed South on I-55 to St. Louis.

Going by Springfield the column was inspired to see so many US flags hanging on vehicles as they zoomed by. However at one overpass, a large group of civilians were again waving flags, but the signs they had were not supportive of the military, and especially them. By the time the last units were passing, rocks were being hurled and balloons filled with urine. Not the welcome and support they had hoped for, and they trusted not a foreshadowing of what was to come.

"Colonel!" came the young voice over the radio again.

"Come back Lead." Returned the Colonel from the twentieth vehicle in line.

"You need to come up here and see this Sir."

"What seems to be the trouble Private?" The column slowed and began stopping in the middle of the four lane highway. "Why are we stopping?"

"Really Sir, you need to see this." Came the voice again.

The Colonel nodded to his driver and they swung out into the passing lane and began moving toward the head of the column. The Colonel felt an uneasiness as he realized there were no cars traveling the other direction, and none were passing the column.

"Keep your eyes open he told his driver" as the Hummer pushed to the front of the caravan.

"What the hell." Was all he could say as they reached the front of the line?

The road had two rows of farm equipment blocking their pathway. As he rolled up close, he was looking at the biggest John Deere combine he had ever envisioned. It was bigger and he imagined heavier that any tank he had ever seen. The only thing it didn't dwarf was a troop carrier, but those didn't have any fire power, just size. The Combine on the other hand had the corn head on and looked like it could do some real damage to any troops it may run into.

Stranger yet, the entire cab of the machine had been covered in steel. From here he couldn't tell how thick, but he knew most of their hand-held fire power wouldn't touch it.

Looking left and right, he counted twenty tractors, all of which had six to eight giant wheels. These were not just tractors. They had John Deere, Massey Ferguson, and some European models he had never heard of written on the sides.

The entire four lanes and the grass divider were blocked. The warning came in the way of a sign, hand painted and simple.

**WARNING-- We will FIGHT for Our Freedom**.

"I need a tank up here." The Colonel said into the mike.

"On my way sir.' came a reply, and he waited for the sound of the rubber covered tracks to reach their position and stop.

"Can you move it?"

"No problem Sir." And the tank moved toward the combine.

Suddenly the sound of another engine joined that of the tank and the head of the combine began to rise.

"Stop there before anyone gets hurt." Came the voice over a loud speaker from the cab of the combine.

The tank stopped. "What do you want me to do Sir?"

The silence seemed to last forever as they sat there, engines running.

"Let me make a call." The colonel pick up his phone. "General, this is Colonel Blake. We seem to have a problem." And he continued to relay the problem at hand. "Yes Sir, talk first."

Putting away his phone, the Colonel climbed out of the Hummer and began approaching the blockage in the road. "Is there a Leader I can talk with before anything gets out of hand?"

"Afraid Not." Came the reply. "Unless you're willing to join us and help maintain our freedom."

"Sorry! Look I have my orders. I need to get by and set up a base in St. Louis. I don't want any trouble, just move and we'll be on our way."

"Then we have a small problem…..Colonel. My orders are to keep you here. You cannot pass unless you move me and that won't happen without a fight."

"Who am I talking to soldier?"

"Just call me Captain, Colonel."

"Ok Captain. If you understand the military as you seem to be implying, you know how badly this could end."

"Tell me something I don't understand sir. You see I volunteered for this task, Did You?"

"What do you mean?"

"Colonel, I'm willing to die for my freedom and that of this country. Are you willing to die trying to take it away? Is that what you serve your country to do?"

"You don't understand, we only need to maintain order."

"No, you don't understand Colonel. I live here, I served from here. I fought in Iraq and Afghanistan. I know disorder and I have seen nothing that warrants this Martial Law action. I only see a government that wants control and will do anything to get that power. Now you have a choice. Will you be the one to draw first blood in what will become a civil war, because that is how this will end if you continue this action? Once again I ask you to join us."

Neither man would get the chance to continue the conversation.

Over the sound of the tank and the combine, nobody heard the engine until it was too late. The explosion sent the Colonel flying back to his convoy and the

John Deere Combine became small pieces of metal strewn around the highway.

Two seconds later the jet became visible as it streaked overhead and down the highway.

"What was that the Colonel yelled at his driver?"

"That was one of ours sir."

"One of ours? Get him on the com.!"

But there would be no conversation. The Colonel became the first military casualty of the Second Civil War just as the Captain had become the first civilian.

That first rocket was joined by a barrage of gun fire from the surrounding bank. Not feeling at all concerned, the Colonel had failed to realize the

significance of the area they stopped. Both sides of the road had a ten foot bank that hide one hundred and fifty militiamen from various Mid-Western states. They had banded together over night to keep this column from reaching St. Louis.

None of the men had expected to be firing upon their own military, but all of that changed in a heartbeat. Sixty civilians and forty soldiers would lose their lives that afternoon just outside St. Louis near Collinsville, Illinois.

The first day of martial law was a day to remember and COLLINSVILLE became the call of the militia.

## News:

Nine-O'clock, day one of Martial Law, Charlie rented a silver Ford Fusion and headed out of New York going west across New Jersey and into Pennsylvania. He gave a call to Jenna and told her where he was and that he loved her. She, in turn, was getting her car and leaving California early the next morning. She would going through Lake Tahoe and Reno with the idea of getting to Denver real late that evening.

It was his hope to reach Chicago in fifteen to seventeen hours including bathroom breaks and food stops. He would sleep for a short time and then on to Denver the next day, where he planned to meet Jenna at the Comfort Inn on 25.

 Saying goodbye, he pushed the pedal a little harder to make better time. However, making time was a fleeting plan as hours passed and the radio filled with the news of the battle of St. Louis.

The news told of the Mid-West Militia's gathering together and attacking the Peace Keeping mission that was traveling there to protect the people.

News of the government roundup of those individuals involved in the attempted assassination plot and the deaths that occurred the day before, told of shootouts, Police Officers dying and hundreds of civilians losing their freedom. Many were rounded up in the Military Martial Law roundup.

All of the news channels were doing their best to make everything sound positive for the government, but you could tell they weren't telling the whole story.

## Bugging Out:

Six hours before Charlie left New York, an old Cessna 310 left a secluded airport just outside Washington. Bill and his family loaded their simple "Bug Out" bags into the plane and quickly headed south away from the city.

Randy wanted to get into the Blue Ridge and Appalachian Mountains as quickly as possible so that he could turn the plane westward. He spent the first hour weaving in and out of the many valleys that intertwined up the eastern side of the country. There were times Bill felt his stomach lurch into his throat as they banked around the bottom of one of the tree covered mountains.

Looking at his family, He felt happy that Michelle and the girls were sleeping soundly in the back of the plane. They had given each of the girls a little Benadryl before they climbed aboard and Michelle had taken a sedative herself right after leaving the airport. Bill looked back and wondered what the next few years would bring for his family.

Slowly Randy began moving the plane farther into the Ohio River Valley and after another hour they had landed at another small airport just outside Indianapolis, Indiana. The airport was run by Scott, a fellow militia member from the Indiana division who had volunteered to meet them when they arrived.

Scott helped Bill's family load into a minivan and within fifteen minutes they were ready to hit the road.

Bill thanked Randy who had decided to take a chance and headed back to Washington; hoping to reach his airport before the sun began to rise.

Scott turned south from the airport and headed the family to his hometown where they would spend the next few days in a small local hotel as the world they all knew and loved fell apart.

## Stop and Go:

Bill and his family were sleeping soundly in Indiana when Charlie came upon his fist road block on Interstate 80 south of Wilkes Barra, Pennsylvania were I-80 and I-81 meet. Traffic began slowing five miles before the I-81 exit, and stopped dead shortly thereafter. This had not been part of his plans, and he wondered what it meant for the rest of his trip. *Just how long will this take he wondered.*

Two hours later he had the answer to his question as he rolled up to the first soldier. It seemed they had everything stopped on both highways in all four directions, north, south east and west.

"Where's your destination?" the soldier asked.

"Eventually Denver.....sir."

"May I see your license and registration for the vehicle and do you have anything to declare?"

"Declare, I'm in America and started in New York." Charlie responded with some sarcasm in his voice.

The young soldier just responded coldly. "Any weapons, drugs, cigarettes, or other items listed as contraband under the statutes of Military and Martial Law."

"Sir, I'm afraid I haven't read up on my statutes of Military or Martial Law lately, but I'm pretty sure I have nothing to declare."

"This is a rental vehicle?"

"Yes sir."

"Please exit the vehicle and step to the curb."

"Why?"

"Just please exit the vehicle and step to the curb."

Charlie realized the young soldier meant business when the soldier put his hand on his pistol handle, and opened the car door for him. Charlie stepped from the car and walked to the curb as three other soldiers began searching his car. They had a dog that stuck its nose into every seat and compartment inside and outside the vehicle while another soldier searched Charlie.

"What are you guys looking for?"

"Weapons! We've had three situations today already. Guys who were stopped on their way to join the rebels in St. Louis. Their cars had over fifteen extra rifles of various varieties hidden inside. One actually climbed out shooting." The soldier nodded at a blood spot on the ground in the middle of the road. "The others are on their way to lock-up."

"So what really happened in St. Louis?" Charlie asked as the boy finished patted him down.

"We really aren't supposed to talk about it, but it seems the locals took on a military convoy heading to protect the city from violence. I've heard the convoy was pushed back and had to take up station thirty miles east of the city limits. We had a reinforcement convoy come by here early this morning. They were loaded."

"Private, shut up." Came an authoritative voice behind them. "Do your job and less commentary."

"Yes sir." The private responded as he snapped to work.

"Sorry." Charlie whispered

The Private nodded acknowledgement and concluded Charlie's stop.

Soon thereafter the first soldier returned. "You're cleared to go. But your route is indicated to stay north on Interstate 80 to Chicago and then take I-90 north to I-25 south in Wyoming the rest of the way to Denver. We placed a sticker in your window that indicates the route. If you are found off route, South of Chicago near I-55 or on any other route that leads toward the St. Louis area, you will be arrested and held as an enemy combatant.  Do you understand these instructions?"

"Yeah." Charlie responded "But, what ever happened to a free and mobile country?"

"That's not my call sir.  We are under Martial and Military Law. Perhaps you can take that up with your Senator, Sir? Have a good day and drive safely." The conversation was over and the soldier backed away from the car indicating for him to move on.

Charlie pulled away from the road block and drove the next hour rolling the conversations he had just had around in his thoughts.

*I wonder what's really going on.*

## Chicago:

Charlie pulled away from the fourth road block he had run into at nine the next morning. He had been on the road for over twenty four hours and needed to pull off the road, but he had an appointment to meet Jenna in Denver. If the rest of the trip continued as the first half had, he would need another full day to get there. No time for rest….not yet.

Charlie took the northern route as he came out of Indiana turning onto Interstate 90/94. He rolled through downtown admiring the skyline, but he was most impressed with the ease he was able to move and surprised by the lack of traffic. He noticed a few military vehicles parked here and there along the road, but for this time of the day, he expected much more congestion.

By the time he reached the western suburbs, he had left 94 behind and was heading North West toward Rockford and Southern Wisconsin. The long day had finally caught up with him so he rolled off the highway at the Des Plaines Oasis just outside of O'Hare Airport. This is the first oasis he had seen that flowed over the interstate from north side to south side. People parking on one side could walk across through the restaurant and restroom areas and exit on the other side of the roadway.

Pulling in because he felt exhaustion overtaking him, he decided to take a nap. He filled his fuel tank and pulled into a secluded spot in the parking lot. He dialed Jenna for an update and tried to relax.

"Hi Baby, it's me. Call me back when you get a chance." He left a message when Jenna failed to answer. *She was supposed to be leaving for Denver an hour or so ago; why wasn't she answering?* Trying to think positive thoughts, he laid back in the seat and let the morning twilight and the lamps that lined the parking lot offer a warming glow to his restless sleep.

A short time later he was brought back to the car by the sound of his phone and the sweet sounds of Blood, Sweat, and Tears he used as his ring tone.

He struggled grabbing the phone as he forced himself awake.

"Hi Honey, sorry I took so long." He said through the haze in his head.

"Hi!" came the sweet sound of Jenna's voice. "Were you sleeping?"

"Yeah, really gone. Are you on the road?"

"Thinks out here are crazy, so I just got in my car. I saw you called, is everything ok?

"Well, Yeah….but." and he began telling of his drive to Chicago. Jenna was not surprised, as her meeting was cut short due to the flight situation and the reported uncertainty in the country.

"Both LAX and San Francisco closed earlier than the others on the west coast. Rumors had been flying around her hotel all last night that airport security was lacking, and some of the TSA officers were siding with the Militia." Jenna's voice slowly became excited. "It seems the problem outside of St. Louis is becoming more wide spread and the people out here are really afraid. Have you heard anything?"

"Jenna!" came Charlie's calming voice. "I need you to relax. Take a deep breath and smile."

Charlie had seen Jenna when she starts to hyperventilate before. "Okay, breathe in through the nose and out through your mouth. *Pause*.....Feeling better?"

"Yeah....yeah thanks Charlie."

"Here's our plan, remember? You leave now. Drive carefully and avoid anyplace that seems a problem. I will do the same from here after I catch some more sleep. We will meet in Denver at the Comfort Suites where we stayed two years ago." Charlie felt her relaxing and felt confident that she was ready to start her trip. "Ready?"

"Yes Charlie, I love you. See you in Denver."

"Drive carefully." Charlie ended. "And I love you too.

Charlie waited to hear the connection end before he hung up. *"Watch over her Father"* Charlie prayed and laid his head back. Sleep came fighting and kicking, but finally he slide off into that place where your thoughts and dreams blend together.

## Wake up to a new day:

BOOM, BOOM "Bill, wake up!!" the voice sounded excited.

Boom, Boom, came the pounding on the bedroom door. "Bill, you need to get moving now!!" Bill recognized the voice of Scott, the man who picked them up at the airport just yesterday "Yeah, Okay," Bill wobbled to the doorway of their motel room. "What's going on?"

"You need to get your family out of here right now."

"What happened?" Bill asked

"It seems we have an infiltrator who told our state authorities where you are and who you are? Grab your bags and head out the back door. Go through the back yard area and turn right. Two blocks down you will find an older blue Ford Focus. It's clean and fueled ready for your family. Here are the keys and good luck to you and your family. I need to leave with mine now." Scott turned to leave running into the darkness.

"Wait, Scott, What's going on?"

"Too much to tell you now, just believe that it's bad. You need to move…..now! Don't wait….now!" Scott waved a quick wave as he ran to his car and sped out of the driveway.

Bill's family was already up and Michelle had the girls dressed.

Bill had spent the night before explaining to his wife what had happened and what his part had been in the assassination attempts. She usually supported Bill in most things, but this had put a strain on their relationship. Michelle's main concern was the girls and therefore she would follow her husband; a man she knew could keep them safe better than any other person she could think of.

"Take the girls, and the first load of bags. I'll finish here and be right behind you." Michelle said "We get out of this and you owe me, big time!"

"I know." Bill responded as he kissed her and headed out the door with the girls and most of the bags. The back door was just a short distance down the inside hallway and quickly they were heading across the back yard of the motel only minutes after being awakened. Bill had the girls wait behind a large tree as he moved out onto the street looking to his right. Two blocks down, there sat a blue car just as Scott had said.

"Come on girls." He whispered, and they moved quickly to the car. Shoving the bags into the trunk and laying the girls on the back seat. Bill turned looking hoping to see Michelle coming onto the street. He waited anxiously standing at the driver's side door for only a minute before deciding.

"Girls, don't move from here, and stay down? Maria, you're the oldest. Keep the door locked until either Mom or I come back." Bill went to the trunk and grabbed a small bag. He withdrew a Glock 45 caliber with silencer and two clips. Checking the clips, he slipped one into the handle, the other into his left hand and began moving down the street, praying that Michelle would step out and they could leave.

His heart jumped when he heard a volley of shots before he reached the tree at the end of the first block.

Running now, he turned at the hiding tree and started across the back yard of the motel going all the way back.

Suddenly, looking up, he realized how much light was on the other side of the building and the flashing effect bouncing off of the tall trees he had just run by. Bill slowed and began moving forward toward the wooden slatted garbage holding bin located near the back door he had come out of just a few minutes before.

Bill heard voices coming around the other side of the bin and he froze.

"See anything?" the first officer asked

"Heck no, give it thirty minutes and we might actually see beyond our arms out here." A second and heavier set officer responded.

Slowly they began moving across the yard area. "Do you think she's dead?" the second officer quizzed.

"Oh yeah, The Sheriff doesn't miss." The voice sounded excited. "I saw her head jump; hit between the eyes and she dropped. I only wish we had waited for the State Boys. They're going to be pissed. Especially when there is no gun on her side."

"Yeah but you know the Sheriff, hates giving up jurisdiction to those guys, and believe me; there will be a gun. Government orders or not, he was going to take her down. Too bad she was alone."

Bill had heard enough. Closing his eyes and taking a full calming breath, Bill reacted. As the two men stepped into the darkest part at the back side of the yard, two shots was all it took. Bill turned and headed into the motel with a new determination that brought back his days in Iraq.

The Officer guarding the hallway was next and he never saw Bill coming. Giving the officers head a quick twist, he was dead before he hit the floor .Bill silently turned the handle on the back door to their room and listened at the crack as the door slowly and silently opened.

Hearing nothing he swung open the door to see two men outside the front door leading to the parking lot. Both men were turned away crouched over Michelle looking at her lifeless body and commenting about how pretty she was.

"How could any man leave something as good looking as this, and run?"

"He didn't." Bill spoke strongly and the two men turned toward him.

The first one, wearing a Deputies cap died immediately as the 45 split his eyebrows. The

Sheriff felt the bullet hit his throat and he hit the ground next to Michelle. Bill walked forward and stared the Sheriff in the eyes as he starred up at him.

Bill knelt down beside Michelle "She was a good women, a great mother and my wife." He said to the Sheriff. "I would never leave her, she was supposed to meet me" Looking at the Sherriff, Bill saw the fear in the man's eyes as he raised the 45. The Sheriff began to choke and Bill heard sirens in the distance.

Bill leaned closer to his wife and whispered "Good bye baby. I'm so sorry. I promise they will be safe."

Bill turned again to the Sheriff. Coughing up blood already, Bill placed another shot in the man's chest. "I need to leave now, but I know you're going to die a real yucky death. Sorry Sheriff, I need to save my children." Bill turned and walked away grabbed the few bags that were left and smiled as he listened to the gasping coughs coming from a man whose life was very short. Bill had wiped out the entire Sheriff's office of this small town.

Later he would feel remorse for the Deputies and their families, but not the Sheriff who decided to act on his own. Bill believed Michelle could have been alive had the sheriff not made that decision.

Bill returned to the car and began driving away as he tried to explain to two very young girls that their mother was not coming.

Not knowing where he would go, Bill headed north on every back winding road he could find that kept him moving.

He drove…..and he drove!

## Des Plaines:

As Bill was winding his way through Indiana, Charlie was sleeping peacefully in his car; that was until he was aroused by the sound of big engines and large equipment.

Opening his eyes, Charlie was surprised to see military everywhere. Trucks, tanks, uniforms and men, lots of men, moving into the Oasis he had chosen just North West of Chicago. The De Plaines Oasis seemed to have become the key military meeting spot on the Interstate.

Tap…Tap came a soft tapping on his window right next to his ear. Jumping and looking up, he saw a young soldier standing beside his car. Immediately he thought of being searched again. So he rolled down his window with regret.

"May I help you? What's going on?" Charlie asked

"Sorry sir, but we are taking over this entire Oasis area and we need you to move on."

"The entire …both sides??"

"Yes sir. We need the control to keep order."

"Has something more been going on?"

"I cannot talk about our activities sir, we just need to clear this overlook."

"Ok, can I get something to eat, or use the restroom?"

After a short hesitation the soldier nodded his head toward the building. "I'll accompany you to the wash room sir, but then you must be heading north."

Charlie and the young man walked to the main building where he saw hundreds of soldiers setting up what looked like some kind of headquarters for the unit. They were cleaning out all of the equipment that had once been a McDonalds and had opened up the entire inside eating area which left an expansive view of the roadway in both directions.

Charlie understood the value of this particular building as it crossed the highway from one side to the other. With it, the military could see anything moving into and out of Chicago from this Northern vantage point, and also have access in both directions with entrance ramps on both ends. He wondered if there were any other overpasses like this being taken over in other states today.

As Charlie slowed his pace to spend more time investigating, he heard comments about St. Louis again, and new comments about a small town outside Indianapolis where a whole Sheriff's department had been ambushed by a group of militia. One had been killed, others were in captivity and more had gotten away and presumed to be heading to Chicago.

As they walked back to the car, Charlie asked the young man, "What do you make of all this?"

"I don't have the ability to have an opinion, sir. I just do."

Charlie climbed back into his car. "Good luck young man. Sometimes even the youngest and lowliest of us can make an intelligent decision that may go against the mainstream, but be the right thing to do. Always think before doing."

"Thank you sir for your advice. Now you must get going. Your tag indicates your route, be sure to follow it."

Charlie nodded agreement and swung his car toward the entrance ramp. He passed a hundred Army vehicles crammed into the small parking area on this side, and realized there were just as many on the other. *A small army!* He thought to himself. *U.S. Army!*

He saw everything as he headed out onto the highway and continued northward toward Southern Wisconsin. Looking at his GPS he pressed the speed limit hoping to make up for some lost time. He believed Jenna would be getting close to Denver and was probably entering the mountains.

"Madison, here I come." He said out loud, talking to himself.

Charlie began to think about what he had just seen, and wondered what Jenna was doing right now.

## Jenna's Trial:

From all she could gather on the radio, traveling toward the south through Arizona and working north would be difficult because you seemed to be heading toward Texas. The Military had a number of road checks along those routes and she knew from talking to Charlie that road blocks were not going to speed up her trip.

South Dakota and Wyoming were supporting Texas, so going way north wasn't going to be any better. So she was working her way up the middle. Lake Tahoe seemed the best choice to reach her destination somewhat on time.

Jenna rolled into Nevada as planned at Lake Tahoe being unsure of what she might find. Everything seemed to be going as expected so far, and as she rolled through town everything was very quiet. The few people she encountered on the street seemed normal, but still very quiet. Normal and quiet was good until she reached the outskirts of town.

A road block was set up stopping and checking cars; only this was not the military or any governmental group. A large group of scruffy looking men with guns, were walking up and down the road, stopping every car going in and out of town. They were demanding money, food or anything else of value from the travelers

Jenna could see a line-up of several cars in front of her; many of which were being damaged by the wandering men. Those men wandering on the roadside were banging on the cars intimidating everyone.

There were piles of cloths, suitcases, coolers and various items from travelers that had obviously been confiscated, checked and discarded on the heap of worthless stuff.

As she moved up the line, she watched as three large men demanded each car pay them for safe passage. If the occupants refused, an even larger man would begin banging on their car with metal piping, this time, leaving huge dents and smashed windows.

This continued until some sort of payment was made or the car was opened and emptied of anything that could hold anything of value.

While the car was being searched, any males were dragged off and beaten while more of the robbers ganged up on the women and harassed them until they finally stopped and let them proceed.

As a single women with nothing to offer, Jenna was getting very scared as her turn was quickly arriving.

Surprising her, a smaller man walked up from the back side of the car, to her window. "Roll down your window Honey." He demanded.

"Don't think so." She responded "What's going on?"

"Hey, just a little fun." He began. "We want to party and need a little cash. You will pay……$100.00 I think to pass."

"I don't have any extra money, and besides I wouldn't give it to you guys if I did."

"That's too bad." He said grinning a clown faced grin. "Maybe we can work something out to lower the payment. Why don't you get out of the car?"

Jenna shuttered. "No, I'm just leaving…now." And Jenna stepped on the gas.

"You're going to hit me" The thief yelled.

"Maybe that's the point." Jenna yelled back as she kept moving. Suddenly the large man carrying the bar swung and hit the roof of her car. Jenna saw the end of the bar enter the cabin through a gaping hole in her roof. In response she hit the brakes and stopped causing the large man to fall and loose hold on the bar.

Five men were on top of her car within seconds yelling at her and banging on her car with hammers and other metal bars similar to the one the large man had. She screamed and yelled for them to stop as she could only expect the worst. Glass was covering the back seat and men were grabbing in at her.

Just as quickly as they all jumped on her car, they unexpectedly began climbing off just as quickly. Jenna watched them running in all directions as the short stocky man who tapped on her window pointed at the sky down the road and began yelling something she couldn't understand.

Jenna watched in surprised as the big man with the pipe dropped to the ground when a splatter of blood ripped out through his back. What was happening?

Abruptly, the whole scene became eerily quiet. Only Jenna and the cars still in line were there and many were climbing from their vehicles. Jenna couldn't figure out what had just happened. Where did the men go?

As Jenna began to view the scene, a sound began to fill her ears. The Thump, Thump, Thump of a rotor suddenly turned into a military helicopter coming around a large boulder farther down the road. The helicopter came flying directly down the road towards them close enough for Jenna to see the side gunner hanging out of the very intimidating military machine.

Unexpectedly, there was the sound of gun fire from the ground directed at the chopper, followed just as quickly, the gunner returned fire and the whole area exploded with combat. Guns were firing from, what seemed, everywhere.

The travelers were screaming and running to their cars. Some never made it as the thieves turned some of their fire at them. Various cars began trying to move around others in the line. People were yelling at each other making things worse. Through the chaos, since Jenna was close to the front, she began moving down the road as quickly as possible trying to move with others, but still on her own..

As she rolled past where the road block had been, she saw two cars pushed off the edge of the road with three bodies on the ground. Feeling lucky as she pulled away, she noticed the little girl crouching along the shoulder of the road.

She sat next a dead women who obviously had been molested and killed earlier in the day. Her clothes were torn open and the body was left fully exposed to the sun, animals and any eyes that looked.

Without hesitation, Jenna pulled her car over as close as she felt comfortable, swung open the driver's door and jumped out. Reaching into the backseat area she grabbed a blanket.

Running toward the crying child, Jenna shook glass off the blanket and in the same move threw it over the women. Scooping the little girl up in her arms, Jenna laid her gently on the front passenger seat, jumped back into the car and sped down the road.

It was then she could hear the child saying "Mommy, mommy," Through the tears and the gun shots that were still flying, Jenna's heart was beating harder than she ever remembered, nevertheless she still felt it breaking for the little child she had just saved.

It was ten miles down the road before Jenna felt comfortable enough to pull over. The helicopter and the smoke had long left her mirrors, and the fear subsided enough for her to consider stopping. The youngster had cried herself to sleep on the seat beside her and from what she could see, seemed to be in good health.

Jenna felt the stiffness in her hands from grasping the steering wheel hard for so long as she stretched her fingers and opened her door. Stepping into the fresh air, she finally noticed the astounding beauty around her and she stretched, reaching high, to calm her racing mind.

Slowly, she began to relax.
Quietly she began to cry, softly at first, but within seconds she was crying hard wishing Charlie had

been there. She was terrified thinking at what she had just survived.

Jenna soon prepared to continue their journey, but before going any farther, Jenna whispered softly to calm her new passenger. "What's you name honey?"

The small girl said "Annie, my name is Annie."

And Jenna smiled. One of her favorite musicals as a young girl had been Annie, so thinking of the orphaned child next to her, she felt the name fit well.

When the car again began to move, a small hand reached out to touch her hip moving her heart and giving her hope that the little girl would be okay.

## Traveling…..over:

The girls had fallen asleep after an hour on the road. Bill hadn't said much of anything and yet the girls never asked once what had happened to their mother. Perhaps it was Bill's mood, or just an inner sense, both of the girl's knew. Their mother was not going with them.

Bill drove north until he reached highway 30 before he decided to turn west. He felt fairly confident that he would not run into anyone that would have too many questions and he could get out of Indiana undetected. The closer he got to the boarder of Illinois, however, he again began using smaller and smaller back roads weaving himself north and south to find the next road heading west.

After hours of traveling, he rolled into one of those small towns in central Illinois you would be through in two minutes unless you had a reason to stop. Bill had two reasons.

Pulling into a small convenience gas station, Bill woke-up the girls and took them in to use the restroom. He left Maria in charge of her little sister as he also used the facilities.

Feeling more comfortable, Bill and the girls moved around the store picking up items they could eat in the car as they kept moving. Small milk jugs, pop, water, bags of snacks, and even a couple of sandwiches found their way into their bag.

Picking up a small cooler and a bag of ice, Bill took everything to the counter and picked up a Chicago Tribune when the headline caught his eye.

"Pretty big stuff going on out there." Came a voice behind the counter.

"What?" Bill responded

"Lots of big news with the St. Louis Massacre and now that thing in Indiana. Pretty bad stuff."

"Yeah." Bill responded "How are things around here?"

"Ahh…we're always quiet around here." The man said as he rang up the items. "You want that paper?"

"Yes, thanks." Bill looked up. "I'll have to read about what's happening out there."

"Did have a military group go through here last night, headed north toward the Interstate." The cashier said as he punched in the amounts for the food. "I think those militias have them spooked."

"Militias?"

"Yeah…the para-military groups through the country. I heard that was what stopped them in St. Louis. Yup…got the government spooked all right."

"How's that going around here? Supportive or not supportive?"

"Illinois? It's like any other state with a large city. Those who live in the city usually follow the government plan, while those of us outside have other ways of doing things. If you know what I mean." The man reached under the counter and brought out a short shotgun he kept there. "Martial Law or not, I take care of myself; as do most of the folks outside Chicago."

Bill shook his head "Thanks for the conversation friend and keep your head down." He grabbed his bags, herded the girls together and walked to his car.

As he started his engine, a squad car pulled in next to his and an officer got out. Readjusting his gun belt, the officer entered the store just as Bill pulled onto the street. Bill felt a strange twinge in the back of his neck he hadn't felt since Iraq.

Bill swung down the second street he passed, turned the car around and pulled behind another vehicle that was sitting along the edge of the road.

Watching the main street he had just left, Bill saw the squad car fly by heading out of town like it was after someone. Bill didn't want to find out who or what the officer was after, although in his heart he knew.

Bill looked in his rear view mirror and saw a long thin farm road heading out of town behind him. Looking ahead he saw the Illinois license plate. After a short time out of his car, Bill turned down that long farm road looking for a place where he could hide while he changed out the Indiana plates he had on his car for the Illinois plates he had lying on the seat next to him. Having decided to try and cross the Mississippi at Dubuque, Bill returned to his thoughts, *Stay off the main roads.*

Two little girls ate donuts, drank their milk and played little girl games on the back seat, again, not saying anything about their missing mother.

## D-Day

The day began as any other day. The sun came up in the East as it had done for the last few million years, and the warmth was drawn into every living thing on the planet, but today was no regular day. Today everything will change.

It became evident early in the morning that something was different. Charlie noticed the military moving everywhere. He had been stopped twice since leaving the Chicago area, not to be challenged, but to wait for military vehicles entering and exiting the Interstate. Finally, an hour went by without anything happening.

The last stop seemed weird when the soldiers seemed disinterested in what they were doing, and moved him along after only a few hurried questions. *Something was up.*

\*\*\*\*\*\*\*\*\*\*\*\*\*\*\*\*

Bill and the girls had just entered Iowa when he noticed the change. He had been laying low following all of the back roads across Illinois, but he knew coming into Iowa he needed to cross the Mississippi River and that meant a bridge. If anyone expected he was on the move, they would be looking for him to cross one of the Iowa bridges.

Moving across Illinois again, he began moving northwest toward Dubuque, a smaller city sitting on the river. He hoped there would be fewer chances of running into full blown military units there, and they could slip through. Hitting US 20 just west of Freeport. Illinois, he headed directly west again through Galena and East Dubuque. However, he had not expected what he found when he reached the Illinois side of the river.

Understanding the girls needed to get out and stretch their legs again and his need to scope out the other shoreline, he rolled up to the bridge on US-20 looking for an overlook. At the base of the bridge he noticed a small sand covered pull-off hidden under the bridge. Suspecting this was a fishing spot, or a place to launch a boat, Bill decided it was the perfect place to take a break. He pulled in.

The girls squealed with joy as they walked the shoreline picking up stones and Bill enjoyed hearing their laughter again. He knew they were dealing with their mother's absence, but they had still been unusually calm the last day.

Bill reached into his backpack and removed a large hunting scope. He laid it on a nearby broken tree limb to steady his view and looking through the scope, he began scanning the far shoreline looking for any signs of military activity. He found it strange to see nothing, no tanks, no trucks, and no men. *"This is strange."* He thought to himself.

The girls laughed again, and he relaxed slightly enjoying the normal feeling of the moment. He decided to remain here on the edge of the Mississippi for an hour so he could continue surveillance. The girls got to continue their activity and Bill got to sit back in the driver's seat of the car and try to forget.

An hour later, they crossed the bridge without anyone stopping them or questioning anything; they just rolled through Dubuque as though it was any other day. Bill grew increasingly concerned. Knowing how bad things should be getting, he knew something somewhere was happening that took all of the military personnel from this area.

Bill set his heading west and drove.

\*\*\*\*\*\*\*\*\*\*\*\*\*\*\*\*\*\*\*\*

Jenna had spent the day before weaving her way through mountains and putting distance between her and the men she had run into the day before. She and her new friend Annie were now rolling into Denver as the new days sunshine was beginning. She was exhausted, hungry and yet, excited to have her part of the journey over. They would find the Comfort Suites, call Sam and settle in to wait for him to arrive. She didn't notice the quiet, the calm, the eeriness of the moment.

\*\*\*\*\*\*\*\*\*\*\*\*\*\*\*\*

Charlie was rolling toward Janesville, Wisconsin
and hadn't been stopped for 2 hours.

\*\*\*\*\*\*\*\*\*\*\*\*\*\*\*

Bill had just reached the far west side of Dubuque,
and was still mulling over the lack of military at the
bridge.

\*\*\*\*\*\*\*\*\*\*\*\*\*\*\*

Jenna pulled into the Comfort Suites on Highway
25 east of the city and found the first available
parking slot.

They all blinked when the bright light spread across
the sky like a huge smoke ring expanding from
some huge giant smoker's mouth. They watched in
awe and wonder as it reached their individual
positions and changed life as they understood it.

## Real Changes:

Charlie was first, as his car was closest to Chicago where the EMP actually exploded. The flash lite up the entire sky, and caused him to look down and squint his eyes. Still, he couldn't see clearly for a few seconds. His car radio immediately died. He had been listening to a small station from Madison that was playing little music, and lots of speculation on the Governments activities but silence is all he had now.

Seconds following the cloud rolling over head, the radio was gone, and his car stopped in the middle of the road. He automatically began reaching for the key to restart when he looked up and realized every other car traveling either direction as far as he could see was having the same problem. The Interstate had abruptly become a parking lot.

Charlie climbed from his car and looked around in disbelief as he automatically began dialing his phone for Jenna.

\*\*\*\*\*\*\*\*\*\*\*\*\*\*\*\*\*\*\*\*

Rolling out of Dubuque, Bill was preparing to turn north toward Minnesota when he noticed that something was wrong. His car sputtered and came rolling to a stop along highway 20 without any warning what so ever. He immediately swore. *Sure stop now when I'm out here in the middle of nowhere!*

He quickly began running through his brain what could be wrong with the car knowing this would certainly put them in danger again; especially if he needed to go back into town. This was when he noticed the ring in the sky and the other cars parked along the roadway just as he was.

Instinctively Bill knew exactly what had happened. His military background brought up terrifying thoughts. "Please don't let this be what I think it is." He prayed out loud to the sky

Picking up his cell phone he turned it on and had nothing……no sound in and no voice out. Cellular communication was dead. Looking around, he realized that everyone he could see was doing similar things to what he was and pointing at the sky. "EMP", he said aloud…again to no one.

\*\*\*\*\*\*\*\*\*\*\*\*\*\*\*\*\*\*\*

Jenna had just pulled into the hotel when her car chugged to a stop. She reached for the key and tried to restart it, but to no avail. "Dead?' she questioned.

She looked at the little girl next to her. "Annie, I'm going inside to get a room. Do you want to wait here or go along?" Seeing the fear in Annie's eyes and they both climbed from the car. Jenna looked around the area and questioned the stagnant silence. Nothing seemed to be moving and like her, a few drivers were outside their vehicles looking around. Some were opening the hoods of their cars and fiddling with wires trying to figure out what happened.

Annie grabbed Jenna's hand tighter as they walked through the front door and saw the commotion happening in the lobby. There were twenty people all standing around complaining about various problems they were having in their rooms; mostly TV and Internet. The poor attendant at the desk was trying to explain that the problem seemed to be worse than just the individual rooms since he also lost all connection with anyone on his computer.

Jenna picked up her phone and tried to call Charlie…no connections. "Excuse me." She yelled at the crowd. "Has anyone tried their phone?"

Two or three people reached for their cell phones and found they too had no service. The attendant picked up the land line for the hotel and it also was dead.

"You might try your cars." She continued. "Mine died as I entered the lot and won't restart." Several turned and headed outside to check their cars only to return shortly with bad news; not one car started.

Suddenly Jenna became the center of attention as others began asking her questions; questions she had no answers for. "Look, I just walked in here and commented about some observations I saw. All I can say is this looks like something more than just the hotel."

Jenna turned toward the large glass windows at the front of the motel. "Have you looked outside beyond the hotel? Everything has come to a stop!"

Suddenly conversations stopped and the guests began acting nervous.

"Look, I'm sure there is an explanation, but until we know what's going on, let's keep calm and think." As no one else was, Jenna seemed to take charge. "If I had a room, I would go there with my family and try to decide what to do next. Obviously this gentleman doesn't know what's going on but I'm sure he will inform everyone as information comes through the office."

Several guests began heading back to their rooms. Others headed outside to their cars and Jenna took Annie to the front desk to see if a room was available.

Befuddled, the young man at the desk said, "May I help you, and thank you; I was getting concerned."

"No problem," Jenna responded. "We just need a room for the night."

"I'm sorry, but since the country went crazy under martial law, we haven't had any rooms. Everyone seems to be heading somewhere. We're all booked."

"Let me suggest something." Jenna responded leaning on the counter. "Do you have anyone coming here tonight from a long distance?"

"Yeah. Actually quite a few."

"I'll guarantee they will not be here. Ninety-nine percent are either sitting on the side of the road someplace or they are sitting on the tarmac at an airport. Even if things change, they will be heading home, not here."

The young man stopped for a minute and looked up." I know you're probably right, but I still cannot give away a room. However, we always keep back two rooms each day for late, late arrivals. We can charge almost any price because they need the room. However, since you helped me out, I'll give you a room for the evening. There are no towels yet, but I can take care of that if you don't mind starting out simple. Besides my computer died a few minutes ago, so I have no way of checking you in. As far as anyone knows, you're not here."

"Mind? Thank you, we'll take the room."

Shortly Jenna and Annie had settled into a spacious room and were sound asleep. That's when the room shook so violently that the pictures shifted on the wall and the TV rattled.

At first Jenna awoke thinking Earthquake, but this had been something different. It was like the entire earth shook for just a second; not the sustained shake of a quake.

*****************

## Disaster:

The first bomb went off in New York City only fifteen minutes after the EMP and leveled most every building including the newly completed Peace Center.

Bomb number two took all of the Washington Monuments, three quarters of the outer city and most of the government with it. The few minutes between the two explosions gave little opportunity for anyone within the Beltway any chance for survival.

Forty minutes later, shortly after Jenna crawled into bed, bombs three and four occurred. Happening, again within seconds of each other, San Francisco and Los Angeles both went up in a flash so strong Casper, Wyoming, Reno Nevada and Denver felt the shocks and witnessed the bright flash of the explosions.

Dallas Texas was the last to go. Having thought they were spared, thirty minutes after the Los

Angeles explosion, Texas rocked from the final blast. Comparatively, it was the worst of the five, as many of the population had already started trying to leave the city and were caught on the overcrowded highways. Millions died.

The briefcase bombs didn't do the massive destruction that would have occurred from a full out nuclear strike, but within the blast zones of the five bombs, few people survived. Those that did survive knew little about where to go and what to do following exposure to high doses of radiation.

The people in Washington who were involved in the beginning of this whole debacle were now gone, leadership in most parts of the country was non-existent and the military was in disarray. It was a perfect time for any outside force to move on the country.

## Invasion:

Russia was first. They had created the EMP that was ignited over Chicago, so they had prepared for the invasion. Within hours of the President declaring martial law, troops were moving across the Bering Sea, plans were set for the EMP strike and the first Russian troop carriers and tanks unloaded on the Southern coast of Alaska near Anchorage

Preparing just off the coast, they entered the Western front across the Aleutian Islands and into Alaska without much confrontation. The small U.S. Military presence based there was mostly communications personnel, and after the EMP they were unprepared for the force that flooded their way. Within a day Russia owned the Alaskan Oil fields and were shutting down production to the lower states and consequently the rest of the free world.

The American and Canadian troops were caught unware as all electronics were gone and the military bases couldn't bring old technology back on line fast enough to prepare for what was coming.

Day two had Russia owning the upper half of Canada and were heading toward Thunder Bay and east toward Toronto in order to enter the U.S. through Minnesota and New York. Any counter attack had to occur soon, or this war would be over before anyone knew it was happening. This was when the first resistance began to slow them down.

The American-Canadian border became blurred as Canadian Resistance fighters and the American militias gathered together to create a civil militia capable of holding off the attack. The Russian troops were not acquainted with Northern Canada and the thick forests covering most of it, so they were susceptible to a gorilla style warfare the Resistance used.

Costing the lives of hundreds of civilian fighters, the Resistance gave the military enough time to re-establish itself. Soon Russia was stalled at the U.S.

China followed the initial Russian attack by hitting Hawaii. Quickly establishing a close Pacific base, they immediately headed to the American coast. Day two, they rolled onto the beaches outside San Francisco and Los Angeles.

Their troops were all wearing full cover protective gear with American flags embossed on them to fool anyone wondering what was happening. Most American survivors of the California bombings thought the troops were friendly and died as they thought they were greeting American troops on shore.

Day three saw China firmly established in California preparing to advance across the Rocky Mountains and out onto the plains.

Day three found Russian troops on the border between the US and Canada preparing to cross the St. Lawrence Seaway east of Niagara Falls, and Minnesota at Thunder Bay and International Falls.

\*\*\*\*\*\*\*\*\*\*\*\*\*\*\*\*\*\*\*\*\*\*\*\*

"Is anyone out there?" came the first crackling words as the old Ham Radio came to life. "Hello, is anyone receiving my calls." Minutes pass.

"Come back on the call" the older female voice responded

"Thank God. I know I'm supposed to use some number or something when I talk on this, but I have no idea what ours is." The young male voice explained.

"Okay." The female voice came back. 'That seems unnecessary at this time. Who is this and how old are you?"

" Please, do you have access to anyone else out there? I have information to pass to anyone in charge.

"What do you mean, in charge?" The voice came back again.

"Look, I'm located in Virginia outside Washington by 75 miles or so. There was an attack that wasted the entire area. I'm trying to find anyone who might be taking control, as our government seems to be gone."

"Again, who am I talking with and what is your location?" Again the female voice sounded, only this time a little more relaxed.

"My name is Chris and I'm in Virginia. Who are you and where are you?"

"Call me Dottie, Chris. I'm outside Chicago.

"Oh, then I don't think you can help." There was a short pause. "Have you heard of anyone in charge; Washington is all but gone. Word around here is that, since Congress was in session, most all of the elected officials were killed."

"Look Chris, I have been looking for another person out there for two days. You're the only voice I have heard. I just wish more people had HAMs, but this technology is so out of date. How are you transmitting when most electrical grids are down out here?" Dottie questioned

"Same here, but my Dad bought a small generator for just this type of emergency last year. He always said the day would come when we would need it. I just didn't think I'd be alone."

"Yeah, my husband and I got ours years ago." Dottie replied. "Who would have thought that there would actually be a time like this."

"Dottie?"

"Yes Chris."

"Have you found any people?" Chris sounded scared.

"Yes Chris, there are people still alive. Hey my friend, how old are you?" she asked.

"Sixteen; my dad and I set this unit up a couple of years ago, but he was the one who always used it" Chris took a breath." I wish I had participated more when he used this thing. I barely know the basics."

"Where is your dad, Chris?" Dottie asked believing she already knew the answer.

"He was inside the beltway when the bomb went off." Chris took a deep breath. "My dad was a Colonel in the Army at the Pentagon." There was another pause. "He didn't come home and I don't think he will be coming home."

How do you know Chris?"

"They're all gone. Washington doesn't exist anymore."

Dottie could hear the assured confidence in his voice. "What are you going to do?"

"I think I'm heading west. It seems more could still exists out there."

"Why not head to the Chicago area Chris. At least we weren't hit by a bomb."

"Sounds like a plan at least" Chris enjoyed the connection. "Where are you Dottie?"

Dottie paused. "Chris here is what I'm suggesting. Wait two days if you have access to food and clean water. That will give your Dad a few more hours to contact you if he can. There is still a chance he may come home. Meanwhile, see if there might be others nearby to come with you. Group together. I would hate to have you heading this way alone. In the mean time I will try to see if I can get anyone else who may be closer than I to assist you along your way."

"Why wait, I could leave in the morning."

"Chris, you have a lot to do. You need to find a wagon or something to carry supplies, water and your equipment. This seems to be the only connection anyone has right now and we don't want to lose this connection. Besides, it has only been a couple of days. Give radiation a few more days to calm down before leaving Washington.

"Yeah, yeah, that makes sense."

Dottie relaxed. "Good Chris, I will call you again tomorrow at this time. Do you have a watch?"

"Yes dad gave me one for my last birthday."

"Does it wind or is it battery operated?"

"Neither, Dad called it an automatic. It winds itself as long as I wear it."

"That is great Chris; never take it off. Are you sure you understand what you're doing tomorrow."

"Yeah, find a wagon, find people and find food and water for my trip."

"Great Chris! Oh, add to your list, a good pair of walking shoes and hiking boots. Oh and fresh socks.

Keep your feet dry." Dottie paused. "Remember you're not alone; if you find anyone else bring them this way with you."

"Thanks Dottie."

"Talk to you tomorrow night 6:00."

"6:00….bye."

## Friends.

Bill and the girls had been walking 3 hours when they crossed the Mississippi back into Illinois. Just after they began walking Bill had seen a strange glow in the eastern horizon, followed shortly by a similar glow from the west. Bill's military background again caused the hair to stand on the back of his neck. He was pretty sure what he had just seen wasn't normal.

When they reached the Mississippi, again, Bill was surprised that there wasn't any military presence at the bridge, but he guessed they were involved with more important things. The EMP would have interrupted all communications and that meant lots was happening, lots that didn't involve him. It meant that he and the girls were clear, for now.

Bill noticed the small tower shortly after crossing the bridge at the Mississippi and hope grew in his chest. A Ham radio tower; a connection to someone else, if they were still using tubes.

Another hour hiking and Bill started to walk up to a white farm house with tall trees, a large barn and the radio tower. The girls were tired and hungry after their long walk and Bill prayed the owners would realize the trouble they were in.

"Stop there." Came a female voice from inside. "What do you want?"

"We were stopped on the road by the EMP hours ago just west of Dubuque." Bill began. "We have been walking back this way for hours and my girls and I need some help."

"Yeah, OK, what do you need?" the voice sounded a little less menacing.

Bill relaxed a little. "We need water if nothing else. My girls need to rest someplace safe and perhaps some food."

After a short silence, "Yeah, I might be able to help." The voice responded. "Sit down where you are."

"I noticed you have a HAM tower." Bill commented as they began to sit in the grass. "Does it work? Can you connect with anyone?"

There was silence.

"Please, I have some friends on Ham, who might know what is happening if you give me an opportunity."

Again there was silence.

Bill heard a door deadbolt unlock and the door began swinging open. "Don't move." The young women said as she stepped onto the porch carrying a small gauge shotgun.

Bill guessed her to be in her early twenties. 'Please be careful with that." Bill said stepping in front of the girls.

"Don't worry, I have lots of experience shooting things. Only difference the targets are usually much smaller than you. I won't miss. Now again, who are you and what do you want?"

"I'm Bill and these are my daughters, Maria and Harriett. As I said before, we only need water and perhaps a place to catch some sleep, somewhere we can feel safe." Pointing at the large barn several feet behind the house, Bill continued. "Your barn would work fine if you wouldn't mind. Is there a well? We could get our own fresh water."

The girl looked closely at Bill and his girls and softened again. Lowering the shotgun toward the ground she said. "The barn isn't water tight, but I don't believe it should be raining tonight. Fresh water can be found from the pump at the cow's watering troughs behind the barn.

"If you have supplies, some food would be good for the girls." Bill asked. "They haven't eaten since this morning on the other side of Dubuque. We've walked this far and they need something to eat. I'll be fine if supplies are short."

"How do I trust you?"

"Honestly honey, I don't know. All I can say is we are here. Either you help, or you don't, but my girls need rest no matter what. Thank you for the use of the barn?" Bill began ushering the girls down the short driveway toward the barn.

The young women took a deep breath and finally shouldered her gun. "Bill, my name is Sadie. The barn has some old hay bales you can open for warmth and comfort. As I said, there is water, but it's from an old hand water pump behind the barn in the old barnyard area. If you don't mind cold water, there is an old water tank you can use for bathing. The sun will be going down soon so if you want a fire, we have a fire pit out there already. Just be careful and keep it small. We don't want to encourage unwanted company nor do we want to start the hay on fire.."

"Thank you, we truly appreciate your hospitality. We will spend the night and be gone in the morning."

Without a response, Sadie turned and went back into the house. Bill, Maria and Harriett went to the barn and shortly had a bed area ready. They went out behind the barn, drew fresh well water for a drink, quickly washed the road dirt off and soon both girls were settled in sleeping nestled between two hay bales and under the silver space blanket Bill kept in his backpack..

Bill had just finished washing when he heard the door to the barn open. Sadie stepped into the barn followed by a middle aged women.

"Hi, my name is Dottie." The women held out her hand. "I actually own this farm. Sadie is my neighbor and looks out for me at times. Her family was on vacation in the east when all of this happened so she's been here most of the time since. I thought you might be able to use some cold chicken, and left over potato salad, I'm sure you're still hungry."

"Dottie, I'm pleased to meet you and thank you for your hospitality." Bill slowly shook her hand and with the hand shake he began relaxing for the first time in many days.

## Farther North:

Charlie watched as the cloud drifted farther and farther east across the sky. This second cloud was different than the first. This cloud came out of the south and he knew everything was changing. The America he knew and took for granted would never be the same. One EMP could be called a mistake, but whatever this second wave was, meant intent and that only could lead to one conclusion.

He looked to the heavens and began a prayer he learned as a boy. "Our father who art in heaven…" and he concluded by offering a short prayer for Jenna's safety. His head told him that she was okay, but his heart told him something very different.

Having traveled north from Chicago, he had gotten a few miles inside the Wisconsin border when everything stopped.

After realizing his car wasn't going anywhere, Charlie began walking back toward Illinois. Why he headed that direction he wasn't really sure, except he knew what was behind him. What might be in front of him to the west, he wasn't sure, but to the south he knew he had passed a truck stop where with any luck, he hoped he could find someone who had information on what was actually going on.

He had walked about a mile when he passed the Beloit, Wisconsin sign on Interstate 90. Up ahead he saw the first signs of activity at an exit that seemed teeming with people. It looked like most everyone traveling north or south around here was making their way to this exit.

Charlie barely entered the area when he saw the old 57 Chevy. A thin and energetic older man was unloading six passengers he had picked up along the highway and seemed ready to head out again as Charlie walked over to the car.

"Are you giving rides?" Charlie called to him.

"Not really. Just depends upon how you look at it." the man responded, " We're just collecting as many as we can before nightfall."

"We, you said! You're not the only moving vehicle?"

"No, our antique car club members are all out on the road."

"I don't get it, How can you be moving?

Look, I'll be back in an hour or so, names Gary, and this is the only red and white 57 Chevy out here, so look for me. To answer your question, think antique, these vehicles have no electronics, and are stored most of the time. No electronics, not moving means nothing electrical was working, so they weren't damaged." Gary began moving, "We have water and a little food available inside the truck stop, relax and we'll try to talk later. Sorry, I need to go in order to beat the dark." Gary pulled away and quickly headed south.

Charlie decided to accept Gary's recommendation and headed toward the small restaurant that connected with the gas station. Planning on spending a couple hours sipping coffee and waiting for Gary's return would develop into something he never expected.

Comfort, food, fresh water and survival would soon over shadow anything else in his life and the lives of everyone around him. Jenna would become an untouchable memory as life changed.

**Change:**

Unknown to Charlie, Jenna or Bill, a War was already being fought; a war that was brought to Canada and America and would be fought for two days exclusively on Canadian soil to the north and California in America.

Warriors congregated from every nearby state to form the civilian army that would battle the enemies to a standstill and give the National Military Establishment enough opportunity to re-establish themselves.

Sadly, once the establishment took over, their perception showed the influence of politicians and political motivations. The war took a staggering turn.

\*\*\*\*\*\*\*\*\*\*\*\*\*\*\*

Jenna and Annie had spent the last twenty four hours in and around their hotel in Denver. Rumors had been passed around about the Chinese and

Russians attacking, but here at the foot of the Rockies they had little concrete information.

Taking a short relaxing moment around the hotel pool, Jenna sat up and watched in horror as the white trails streaked skyward. Grabbing Annie, she ran into the hotel. She knew what she had seen and she had the understanding the end results a nuclear war presented.

Running into the hotel there were others who were talking about the "white steaks in the sky" but failed to understand their significance. Jenna grabbed water and anything that looked reasonably nutritious, shoved it into a shopping bag and herded Annie into the basement. Settling her and the supplies into a solid concrete corner Jenna told her "Stay here and don't leave. I promise, I'll be back."

Jenna began running down hallways banging on doors and warning anyone who would listen that they had twenty minutes to find shelter.

"Grab anything you can to eat or drink and head to the basement. We launched our missiles and that means others are either already headed this way, or they will be soon. Please, head to the basement!!"

Jenna ran through the main lobby and grabbed more water bottles, candy and anything she could from the hotel store area.

"What are you doing?" A voice was yelling at her. "Stop!"

"I'm not stopping." She yelled back. "I just saw a number of missile launches out there. We need to quickly prepare."

The siren started blaring outside as Jenna focused a band of ten people into the basement. She closed the door and settled into the corner next to Annie and waited. She began to pray. Annie joined her and soon the small band hiding and waiting for the inevitable in the basement of a Denver hotel were all praying for God's grace and protection.

\*\*\*\*\*\*\*\*\*\*\*\*\*\*\*\*

Two states away, Bill and the girls were listening to Dottie's Ham radio and heard the news. They too grabbed food and water, as well as Dottie and Sadie and headed for the storm shelter Dottie had for weather emergencies. They made it just in time for the first blasts to hit Chicago, Houston and Philadelphia.

****************

Charlie felt the earth shake through his entire body. More than just a feeling, this was an immediate dread that only comes from realization that something bad just happened even though you don't yet know what it is.

A few seconds' later people were running into the shopping area of the truck stop screaming. Some were declaring "the End of the World" terrified and not thinking. Charlie knew what had occurred and reacted.

He assumed the explosion took Chicago, and time became an issue immediately.

Charlie knew they had five minutes at the most to prepare for this facility and everything else around them to cease existing

Charlie grabbed two men near bye who looked like they were still under control, "Grab water and anything that looks like food and head your families to the bathrooms. We don't have any time, so move."

The two men began grabbing and Charlie noticed they were encouraging anyone they could to join the plan. Charlie ran to the door and scanned the one hundred people who had been dropped here. Most were crying, frozen with fear. He knew he could not save them all and realized he didn't know if he could save anyone, but he would try to save those he could.

Charlie turned to those inside the shop and yelled. "Move to the bathrooms. If we have any chance, we need to get there. Those walls are inside and strong, they should withstand what's coming.

Grab anything for food and water and go. Out here you die!

Sadly Charlie only saw a fraction of those inside react as he began grabbing bags and bottles working his way into the bathroom area.

As he closed the door behind him, he heard the final screams as the outer ring of the nuclear blast that leveled Chicago hit seventy-five miles away.

 The shattering glass and flying debris killed everyone left outside and within seconds the silence beyond the bathroom door left the few inside the room stunned with disbelief.

Charlie sat on the floor put his face in his hands and took a deep breath. He realized when the door opened again, nothing would be the same. He realized just how lucky he was to have been here and not where he was earlier in the day, or just an hour ago.

Through what now were tears, Charlie prayed again.

On this day, America changed. The World changed. Most of the world population died within a matter of minutes, and over the next decade, millions more would die from starvation, exposure and sadly, man being cruel to man.

The next year would be spent in much the same manner in any part of the World you would observed. Survivors lived as much underground as possible; only sending out exploratory groups to find food, bottled water or materials for communication with others who may be survivors.

The natural world had taken a huge hit. Most vegetation was gone for many miles around the blast areas and remained that way for a year. Temperatures dropped as the cloud cover increased and remained in place for three months.

Year one concluded with a realization that human life was back in the earliest years where survival depends upon one's ability to adapt.

The second year after the desolation, the people began developing outside settlements. Moving outside of their protective holes in the ground, developing more extensive exploration, gathering together in survival groups and slowly a new world began to develop.

A New World,     A New Life,     A New Story


THE END.........or is it the beginning?